W9-BAS-455

BOEING 777

BRUCE CAMPION-SMITH

IAN ALLAN Publishing

Contents

Acknowledgements

This book would not have been possible without the kind and generous assistance of the people who make the Boeing 777 and the airlines that fly it.

First, I am indebted to Kirsti Dunn and Liz Verdier, of Boeing's Public Relations Department, who so kindly took time to show me around the Everett plant and the aircraft itself.

Others at Boeing were also of great help: Ken Higgins, John Monroe and Nick Milham; Ken Dejarlais, of the company's visual communications department, provided many of the pictures that appear in the book. Errol Weaver, Boeing's Canadian contact, provided invaluable help. Thank you also to John Kvasnosky, Managing Editor of Boeing's Airliner magazine which was a useful source of technical detail about the aircraft's development and systems.

Thanks also to Honor Verrier, Peter Jones and Barry Gosnold at British Airways; Tom Fredo at All Nippon Airways; Morris Simoncelli at Japan Airlines; Gordon McKinzie and Joe Hopkins at United Airlines; Peter Gardner at Cathay Pacific Airways; Rick Kennedy at GE; Mark Sullivan at Pratt & Whitney; Mark Baseley and Robert Stangarone at Rolls-Royce; Jim Veihdeffer at Honeywell. And finally, thanks to two special people on the homefront: David and Lori.

Front cover:
The front end of Boeing's own 777
Austin J. Brown/APL

Back cover:
Pictured during take-off at Paine Field, Everett, Wa and bearing the airline's 50th anniversary livery, is the first of 11 Boeing 777 bound for Cathay Pacific. *Boeing*

Title page:
China Southern has ordered six 777s. *Boeing*

First published 1997

ISBN 0 7110 2504 5

Code: 9707/B3

Published by Ian Allan Publishing

an imprint of Ian Allan Ltd, Terminal House, Station Approach, Shepperton, Surrey TW17 8AS.
Printed by Ian Allan Printing Ltd at its works at Coombelands in Runnymede, England.

1. A Renaissance Aircraft

With two underwing engines and a wide-body fuselage, it can be mistaken for a 767 when seen from a distance across an airport ramp. It is only close up that one realizes that the Boeing 777 is a jet unlike any other.

It is the largest twin-engine jet ever built; the landing gear is the largest ever designed for a commercial aircraft. It is powered by new advanced engines — the most powerful yet. The area of its horizontal stabilizer alone is equal to the entire 737 wing. In fact, the overall dimensions of the 777 fall just short of the Boeing 747-400, the biggest commercial jetliner flying.

The 777 is also Boeing's first all-new commercial jetliner since the 757 entered service in 1983 and only the seventh model since the 707, the airliner that helped launch the jet age. Boeing has built some of the best-known aircraft in the sky — the Clipper, Stratocruiser, 707, 727, 737, 747, 757 and 767. Each marked a technological step forward and the 777, the company's last all-new design this century, is no different.

The 777 is an aircraft built for the digital age. It was designed by ultra-sophisticated computers. It is guided by a computerized fly-by-wire flight control system, a first for a Boeing aircraft. A digital 'brain' manages the advanced avionics and electronics. Composite materials are used extensively throughout the aircraft to reduce weight and it has new features to make maintenance easier and to cut downtime. It was the first jet approved to fly long, trans-oceanic routes from its first day in service.

But the 777 is more than just a new aircraft. With its introduction, the jet has become the showcase of a dramatically different way of designing and building aircraft for the Seattle-based manufacturer. When the 777 was launched, the risks for Boeing were significant. It would be an unproven engine on an unproven aircraft, a combination that would seem to invite delays. As a multi-billion dollar gamble that would in large measure decide the future of the company, the development of the 777 was in many ways reminiscent of the development of the jet that Boeing remains

Below:
The 777, seen here in the middle, was Boeing's response to the demands of airlines for an aircraft sized between the 420-passenger 747-400 and the 767, which can carry 218 passengers. *Boeing*

best known for, the 747. Back at the time of the 747 roll-out, Boeing was battling Lockheed and McDonnell Douglas for orders. Today, the battleground is much different. Boeing, long the undisputed master of the skies, is now up against the European consortium Airbus Industrie in the war for market share. After more than a year in service, the 777 is a success, both in the air and in the order-book — by 1 January 1997, Boeing had 318 orders for its big new jet. Its popularity is easily explained by its economics. A 777 can carry passenger loads approaching that of an early 747 but with two fewer engines and a two-pilot cockpit instead of three. And it can fly routes once reserved for trijets and four-engined jumbos.

Birth of an Aircraft
It was late 1986 when Boeing began assessing market preferences and talking to airlines to find out what its next aircraft should be. At the time, the manufacturer already boasted a complete line-up of aircraft — an upgrade of its 737 had boosted sales of this hugely successful workhorse; sales were picking up of the 757 and 767, the twinjets for domestic and intercontinental flights; and the development of the 747-400 was well underway.

Missing from the line-up, though, was an aircraft sized to fit the niche between the

Above:
The 777 was designed for a lucrative market to replace hundreds of aging Lockheed L-1011s and DC-10s. The stretched version of the twinjet will even replace older models of the Boeing 747. *United Airlines*

Top right and right:
The 777's big competitors in the market are the A340 and A330. As Boeing debated whether to go ahead with its new wide-body project, Airbus Industrie already had a significant headstart and was taking orders for its two new jets. *Airbus Industrie*

269-seat 767-300 and the 420-seat 747-400 which had the capability for future growth, both in passenger capacity and extra range.

For Boeing, the obvious, and least costly, solution was to develop a derivative of its 767, stretched to fill the medium-lift market, roughly defined as 250 to 400 passengers with a range of 4,200nm. The 767 had already been stretched by 21ft to create the 767-300, which can carry 269 passengers in two classes, about 40 more than the 767-200. But between 1986 and 1988, the preliminary design process looked at further changes to the aircraft that included a stretched fuselage, a new wing, new empennage and

more powerful engines that produced in the range of 74,000lb to 80,000lb thrust. They even considered a strange looking double-decker design — nicknamed the Hunchback of Mukilteo, after a nearby town — that mated a portion of 757 fuselage to the top of the rear fuselage of the 767.

But when Boeing sounded out the airlines for their opinions of these different designs, it was clear the concepts were not what the carriers were looking for. The airlines told Boeing they wanted a wide-body aircraft with the efficiencies of the 767 — two engines, two crew and low operating costs — but able to carry more passengers, longer

distances. They wanted flexibility in range, routes and interior configurations, a jet that could be used on high-density domestic routes as well as oceanic journeys that have typically been the domain of three and four-engine aircraft.

In 1989, rumours abounded that Boeing may use the Paris Air Show as the venue to announce the launch of a new model. Indeed, a Boeing official confirmed that the aerospace giant was taking a close look at the 300-350 seat market. But he said there had been no decision whether the company would go with a stretched 767 or an entirely new design.

777 General Arrangement

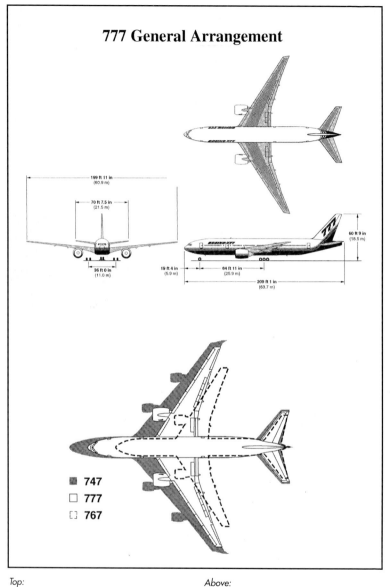

199 ft 11 in
(60.9 m)

70 ft 7.5 in
(21.5 m)

36 ft 0 in
(11.0 m)

60 ft 9 in
(18.5 m)

19 ft 4 in
(5.9 m)

84 ft 11 in
(25.9 m)

209 ft 1 in
(63.7 m)

■ 747
□ 777
[] 767

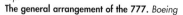

Top:
The general arrangement of the 777. *Boeing*

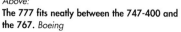

Above:
The 777 fits neatly between the 747-400 and the 767. *Boeing*

Above:
The 777 forever changed the way that Boeing built aircraft and introduced a new design process that will be used for new models for years to come, including the redesign of the 737. *Boeing*

Below:
Boeing invited the input of airlines into the design of the new jet. Cathay Pacific Airways pushed for a wider fuselage to near 747 dimensions that would allow 10-abreast seating. *Rolls-Royce*

At the time Boeing was debating the decision whether to go ahead with a new wide-body, its two competitors had already spotted the niche and were busy selling aircraft to fill it. McDonnell Douglas was offering the MD-11, a new version of its DC-10. Arch-rival Airbus Industrie had two aircraft under development — the 328-seat A330 twinjet and the longer-range A340.

Up for grabs was a huge market to replace aging three and four-engined jets. For example, Cathay Pacific Airways needed a replacement for its Lockheed L-1011 TriStars and British Airways was on the market to replace its L-1011s and DC-10s. And in 1988, United Airlines was seriously looking at the A330 to replace its fleet of venerable DC-10s, which were approaching a quarter century of flying. Boeing estimates that by 2015, airlines will need 3,473 aircraft in the intermediate size category. This category, which includes the 777, will be the fastest growing segment for carriers looking to meet growth and replace aging jets.

If Boeing decided to go ahead with a new aircraft, it would be five years late entering the market. But without an aircraft to offer airlines, the company would be forfeiting the market altogether and missing out on billions of dollars in sales.

Public statements aside, Boeing had heard the airlines' message. After several false starts looking at variations of the 767, there were growing signals that the new jet, known as the 767-X, would be born from a clean sheet

of paper, or in this case a blank computer screen. In the early part of 1989, Boeing began calling several airlines to tell them about its development of a new wing design. The 767 wing was not large enough to accommodate a bigger aircraft, a constraint in trying to satisfy the airlines' needs with a 767 derivative. One of the first invited to see the new, highly efficient airfoil in the wind tunnel was Gordon McKinzie, of United Airlines, who at the time was evaluating the A330. The new aircraft moved one step closer to reality on 8 December 1989, when Boeing's Board of Directors authorized the Boeing Commercial Aircraft Group to formally offer the 767-X to the airlines. The New Airplane Division was established in Renton, Wa, to oversee the aircraft's development. The delay in entering the market would mean lost sales. But it also enabled the company to miss the worst of a recession that crippled airlines worldwide. And more importantly, Boeing used this time to start a process unique in its history — they asked the airlines to help design the new jet.

airlines was to produce a service-ready jet without the costly snags and delays that usually accompany a new design. It was also an attempt to avoid a painful repeat of the launch of the 747-400, which got off to a rocky start when initial deliveries were delayed and then was plagued with lingering complaints about quality.

Working Together

Boeing convened what has become known as the 'Gang of Eight' and invited planners from United Airlines, American Airlines, Delta Air Lines, British Airways, Japan Airlines, All Nippon Airways, Cathay Pacific Airways and Qantas Airways to take part in the design process. At the time, Boeing had pretty well defined the new aircraft as a large 767. But the company wanted the major airlines to help it determine the features of the new aircraft.

On the face of it, this consultation seems like a rather simple concept. But it represented a major change in the way that Boeing had been doing business. The 777 was designed with extensive customer involvement, more than any aircraft that Boeing had built before. In December 1989, United Airlines signed a memo of understanding with Boeing stating that if the airline signed on as the launch customer, it would want to be more involved in the design process. The goal for Boeing and the

Gordon McKinzie, United Airlines' Manager of Boeing Acquisition Programs, calls the 777 a 'renaissance airplane' because of this new working together relationship. In the past, airlines would attend briefings, visit mock-ups and get a thick set of specifications for the aircraft then wait years for delivery. But with the 777, the relationship changed between Boeing and its customers and will likely never be the same again. The Gang of Eight met with Boeing staff three times, with each session lasting several days. They contributed their real-life experiences in terms of routes, traffic loads, service frequency and climate. In separate sessions, the airlines brought in their own experts. Mechanics made the aircraft easier to maintain, pilots gave their input on avionics and flightdeck design and flight attendants told Boeing how to improve the galley design and overall passenger service. Boeing learned from the airlines what would work and what wouldn't.

At the time of the first meeting, Boeing had defined the new aircraft as a large 767

with two engines, similar in size to a DC-10 but cheaper to fly. Designers were not wedded to the idea of a two-engine jet but it made economic sense. During the latter part of the 1970s, Boeing was looking at the development of a three-engined model, similar in configuration to the DC-10, that was commonly called the 777. But designers became convinced that aircraft no longer needed more than two engines to take off and climb safely and achieve long-range flight. Improvements in design and aerodynamics and powerful high-bypass engines gave twins the capability for long-range operations, as was demonstrated by the 767 and 757.

The airlines had agreed on a number of items. They wanted the flightdeck patterned after the 747-400, not the 767 as Boeing had planned in the hopes that it would share pilot type ratings with the 757 and 767. In the cabin they asked for interactive video displays, flexible interiors, and better ventilation.

In maintenance, the airlines argued for built-in test equipment and a maintenance access terminal on the flightdeck. In United's experience, mechanical problems had been accounting for 35% of all delays. An easily maintained aircraft would mean fewer delays.

Boeing also considered a new fuselage with a wider cross-section. But just how wide was the subject of considerable discussion. The airlines complained that the existing nine-abreast seating suffers in seat width to keep aisles reasonably wide. Cathay Pacific

urged Boeing to widen the cabin by nearly a foot to near 747 dimensions. The result is a cabin cross-section 5in wider than the DC-10, enough for wider seats and aisles and nine or 10-abreast seating. All Nippon's desire for a slightly longer aircraft resulted in a couple of frames being added to the design to increase the aircraft's length by about 4ft. By the autumn of 1990, the basic configuration of the 777 had been largely decided. Together with new engines and a new wing, Boeing had the makings of a new aircraft. Designers had capitalized on the delay by making their aircraft bigger and more flexible than the McDonnell Douglas or Airbus aircraft. The cabin of the new twinjet would be wider and have more headroom. It would also incorporate technological advances like fly-by-wire flight controls, an advanced digital flightdeck and make extensive use of weight-saving composites.

It would seat between 305 and 440 passengers depending on configuration and would be offered at gross weights from 506,000 to 632,500lb, allowing airlines to pick an aircraft best suited for their flying,

whether it would be for regional or domestic routes or long-range flights.

Launch

An autumn weekend in 1990 proved fateful in the evolution of the 777. United Airlines was making its final selection for a wide-body aircraft that would serve it well into the next century. Representatives from Boeing, McDonnell Douglas and Airbus Industrie and staff from the engine makers — General Electric, Pratt & Whitney and Rolls-Royce — all gathered at United's Chicago headquarters to make their pitch. Despite United's active involvement in the 777 design process, it was far from assured that the multi-billion dollar order would go to Boeing. Also in the running were the Airbus A330, A340 and MD-11. In all, there were 33 combinations of engines and airframes for United to consider. But after a marathon 70 hours of negotiation, United executives had good news for Boeing.

On 15 October, United announced that it had ordered 34 Pratt & Whitney-powered 777-200s and placed options for 34 more. Boeing would need hundreds more orders for

777 Range Capability From London

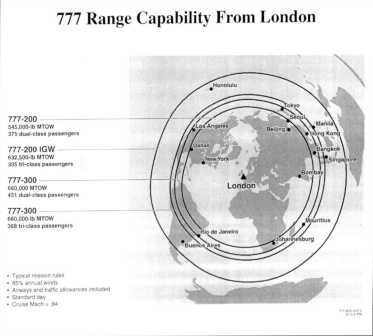

777-200
545,000-lb MTOW
375 dual-class passengers

777-200 IGW
632,500-lb MTOW
305 tri-class passengers

777-300
660,000 MTOW
451 dual-class passengers

777-300
660,000-lb MTOW
368 tri-class passengers

- Typical mission rules
- 85% annual winds
- Airways and traffic allowances included
- Standard day
- Cruise Mach = .84

Honolulu

Tokyo
Seoul
Manila
Los Angeles
Beijing
Hong Kong
Dallas
Bangkok
New York
Singapore
Bombay
London
Mauritius
Rio de Janeiro
Johannesburg
Buenos Aires

777-6CC-243 C
B-14-6 PW

Above:
The range of the 777 out of London. *Boeing*

its new jet to recoup the tremendous development costs, estimated to be in excess of $5 billion. But for now, the 777 was born.

United Airlines, though, wanted assurances that its demands and wishes would be listened to. The outcome was a simple set of guidelines entitled 'B777 Objectives', a hand-written agreement spelled out on a single sheet of yellow legal-sized paper and signed by executives from Boeing and United. It promised that the aircraft would offer from its first day in service the greatest dispatch reliability in the industry, the greatest passenger appeal and would be an aircraft

that is user friendly and in which everything works. This note, which now hangs framed in the 777 offices, set the tone for the process that followed.

Two weeks after the order was announced, Boeing's Board of Directors formally approved launching the twinjet into production and the New Airplane Division was renamed the 777 Division. In a statement, Frank Shrontz, then Chief Executive Officer of The Boeing Company, said: 'The Boeing 777 will set a new standard for aircraft around the world.'

Boeing had plans for a family of 777 aircraft. The base model, or A-market jet, would compete with the Airbus A330 to replace old DC-10s and L-1011s. A higher gross weight and longer-range model, called the B-market jet, would fly long, thin routes starting in early 1997. It would compete against the A340 and the MD-11. A stretched version of the A-market model able to carry 368 to 550 passengers was planned for 1998.

The terms A-market, B-market and C-market refer to wide-body aircraft ranges. The A-market is 3,000 to 5,000 plus nautical miles to accommodate domestic or regional routes; the B-market designates ranges of between 5,000-7,000nm for international routes and C-market is 7,000nm or more. The range of the A-market version means it can serve city pairs such as New York-San Francisco, London-New York and Chicago-Honolulu. The

extended range B-market jet can fly such trips as Chicago-Seoul and Dubai-New York.

United had insisted that Boeing guarantee the A-market aircraft would be able to fly from Denver to Honolulu from the day it entered service. This single route established a number of tough performance requirements. United wanted the jet to carry a full load of passengers out of the 5,000ft airport on a hot summer day and have the range to make it to Hawaii flying into the worst winter headwinds. In the event the 777 lost an engine en route, Boeing had to show that the minimum, single-engine altitude would still clear the highest elevation en route, at about 16,000ft over the Rockies.

But perhaps most importantly, the Denver-Honolulu route required the 777 to be approved for long oceanic flights from its first day in revenue service, an approval which was unprecedented.

Within just a few months, United had set up a 777 development team in Boeing offices. The airline had always had a factory representative working at the company to look after quality control on aircraft deliveries. But this new office, led by United's Gordon McKinzie, was in the heart of the 777 engineering department, an indication of just how involved the airlines were to become in designing the aircraft.

A team from All Nippon Airways was the next on site shortly after the airline became the second carrier to purchase the jet with its order for 15 777s and options for 10 more on 19 December 1990. In June 1991, Thai Airways International announced it would be taking six 777s equipped with Rolls-Royce Trent 800 engines, becoming the launch customer for the engine. A big order followed in August when British Airways confirmed it had ordered 15 777s and taken options for another 15, all powered by the GE90. The year was rounded off with orders from Japan Airlines for 10 777s and options for 10 more and Lauda Air of Austria for four longer-range 777s.

The Gang of Eight became the Gang of Four: United, All Nippon, British Airways and Japan Airlines remained involved in the design process, each with their own engineers working on site, side by side with Boeing staff. In all, about 300 airlines employees temporarily located to Boeing facilities and participated in design/build teams. McKinzie admits this new relationship, which had airline staff sitting in on design meetings, was initially awkward for both sides. But that soon changed as the two sides grew to trust and be honest with each other. 'After a while, they wouldn't start a meeting without us,' he said. He cites one incident to demonstrate the effectiveness of the Working Together relationship. Boeing had decided to use silver-plated wires on the 777 to carry the signals from fuel tank sensors. United staff were worried because silver corrodes quite easily, creating erratic fuel readings. Because the corrosion is hidden beneath the wire sheath, troubleshooting can be difficult. During a meeting with a Boeing engineer, McKinzie tossed on the table a corroded, silver wire bundle that had been pulled from a DC-10 fuel tank undergoing overhaul. McKinzie's complaint: the wires should be coated with corrosion-resistant nickel. Within hours, Boeing had opted to go with the more reliable nickel wiring.

That was just one of hundreds of airline ideas that were incorporated in the design. Others included relocating the fuelling panel to a lower part of the wing so the airlines would not have to buy new fuelling equipment, and increasing the size of push buttons so maintenance crews working in cold climates could easily open an exterior access panel without removing their gloves. They even redesigned the passenger reading lights so a burned out bulb could be changed in flight. British Airways pushed for an increase in the maximum take-off weight to 535,000lb from 515,000lb for the A-market aircraft. The British carrier also suggested changing the arrangement of the rear galley to make space for two lavatories from elsewhere in the aircraft. Moving the lavatories aft opened up room for four more seats.

A Paperless Aircraft

In a corner of the Boeing factory in Everett, Wa, is the empty fuselage section of a Boeing 747-400. It was never meant to fly; rather its role was to test how the work of the designers and their drawings came together in production.

Full-size metal and wood mock-ups like this one were a chance to catch design mistakes before the aircraft entered full production. The many parts of an aircraft — wire bundles, hydraulic lines and control cables — were installed on the mock-up to ensure they fitted properly and did not interfere with other parts.

For all the accuracy of the drawings, inevitably, there were unfortunate surprises. Often, the assembly line became the final testing ground as designs were further corrected on the first few aircraft. But reworking a design at this stage was expensive, inefficient and could delay production. Past experience had shown that part interference — cases when two parts overlap — and trouble fitting parts together were the biggest problems in manufacturing.

Left:
First flight: the centre fuselage section complete with wings is carried by crane to the final body join area where it will be mated to the forward and aft sections of the fuselage. *Boeing*

Below left:
Thanks to computer design, the components of the 777 went together easier than on any other Boeing aircraft. By late 1996, the factory was producing three-and-a-half 777s a month, a rate it is planning to increase to seven a month by late 1997. Boeing also wants to cut the time between order and delivery to 10 months, down from the current 16 to 18-month wait, to better respond to airline demands. *Boeing*

Below:
The first 777 in the final assembly position. Here electrical, hydraulic and pneumatic systems are activated and the engines and the APU are installed. In the background is the final body join position where all of the major aircraft structures are brought together for the first time. *Boeing*

For Boeing, the solution was computer-aided design; the 777 was a paperless aircraft, designed entirely on computer without blueprints or the traditional wood and metal mock-up. The company had been experimenting with computer-aided design and computer-aided manufacturing (CAD/CAM) technology for some time. From that experience, the engineering department was confident by 1989 that it could significantly reduce costly rework by digitally preassembling the aircraft on computer. CAD had been used before but the 777 marked the first time the company designed and preassembled a jet solely on computer.

Boeing turned to an IBM/Dassault computer system called CATIA, short for computer-aided three-dimensional interactive application system. To work on a project the scale of the 777, Boeing made enhancements to several areas of the system, such as data management and visualization. Because it was such a big change, it was decided to test CATIA by building a mock-up of the 777's nose section. Crowded with equipment racks, air conditioning ducts and wiring bundles, this is one of the most complicated sections of any aircraft. The test demonstrated that CATIA worked and provided the confidence to proceed without a full-size mock-up.

CATIA enabled engineers to see aircraft parts as three-dimensional solids on the computer. The parts were then preassembled on the computer, creating a digital mock-up of the aircraft which revealed misalignments and interference problems.

When a problem was discovered, staff could move the part or redesign it.

The payoff was on the factory floor as workers found many of the aircraft parts fitted together precisely, eliminating the need for additional work. When the first aircraft's major body sections were joined and aligned by laser, it was only 0.023in, about the thickness of a playing card, from perfect alignment from nose to tail. Most aircraft line up within a half inch. Boeing's goal was to reduce change, error and rework by half, a goal it exceeded, saving millions of dollars in costly rework. The computers even added a human touch — a digital mechanic nicknamed CATIA-man who could climb around inside the computer aircraft to show how difficult it would be for a real mechanic to access and repair parts of the aircraft. The original CATIA-man had the abilities of a super-hero and was a little too agile; Boeing made changes to make him more representative of a typical mechanic.

To use this technology, design/build teams were established — 238 teams in all — to develop the components of the aircraft, everything from wing structures to fuel and wiring. This approach, a first for Boeing, brought together all of the different specialities involved in aircraft development — designers, tooling, engineers, finance,

suppliers and customers — to jointly create the parts and systems.

In the past, aircraft had been designed in sequence. Structures engineers would do their design work, followed by systems engineers and on down the line. Each group completed their designs in isolation and then 'threw it over the wall' for the next group to work on and make changes. Then the designs would go to manufacturing and tooling groups who had to figure out how to build it. By this stage, there had been hundreds of costly and time-consuming revisions, making it a laborious and often inefficient process. CATIA and the design/build teams enabled the groups to work in parallel. Linked by computer, each design/build team could work on their own part of the aircraft while staying informed about the overall progress of the design.

The designers were connected by an extensive network of computer work stations, about 1,700 alone in the Puget Sound area around Seattle, tied into eight IBM mainframe computers, the largest mainframe installation in the world. This cluster is also linked to computers in Japan, Wichita, Philadelphia and other sites where 777 parts are manufactured.

ETOPS

With the decision that the new aircraft would be a twin, Boeing now faced another hurdle — winning regulatory approval for the 777 to fly long routes over water up to 3hr flying time from the nearest airport.

The Boeing 767 had pioneered this type of flying — called extended-range, twin-engine operations (ETOPS). ETOPS refers to twin-engine operations where a portion of the flight is more than 60min away from an airport if the aircraft has to divert with one engine shut down.

Typically, an aircraft earned the privilege to fly such flights only after its reliability was proven on thousands of shorter flights, a process which usually took two years. Boeing, however, promised that the 777 would have approval to fly ETOPS routes on its first day in revenue service. It was an ambitious commitment. If successful, the 777 would be the first commercial jetliner in aviation history to enter service with 180min ETOPS approval. Without ETOPS approval, though, the 777 would be restricted to routings no more than an hour from an airport and the jet's potential to fly from 4,600 to 7,600 miles on routes such as New York to London, Denver to Honolulu or Tokyo to Sydney would be wasted.

Just over a decade earlier, twin-engine operations across the North Atlantic were virtually non-existent. The regulations were a carry-over from the days of sometimes unreliable piston-powered aircraft. Some in the industry even quipped that the

Stratocruiser, equipped with four 3,500hp Pratt & Whitney Wasp Major engines, was 'Boeing's best three-engined aircraft'. Today's high bypass jet engines are 10 times more reliable than the piston engines of the 1950s, according to Boeing.

It was the introduction of twinjets like the Airbus A300 and Boeing 767 and 757 in the mid-1980s that convinced regulatory authorities to permit twin-engined aircraft on routes one to three hours from an airport, as long as airlines met stringent equipment and training requirements. For passengers, ETOPS means shorter travel times and more nonstop service to a greater number of cities. It has also resulted in more flights since twins cost less to operate — 5%-9% lower operating costs — than the three and four-engined jets that had dominated the oceanic routes.

Now twin-engine flights are routine, thanks to the reliability of today's jet engines. In fact, US airlines now have more twin operations across the Atlantic than three and four-engined flights. Around the world, there are more than 11,000 ETOPS flights by Boeing twins every month — nearly 400 a day over the Atlantic, western and central Pacific, Caribbean and Indian Ocean.

Engine reliability is expressed in terms of in-flight shutdown rates (IFSD), measured by the number of engine shutdowns for every 1,000hr of flight operations. To qualify for 120min ETOPS approval, an engine must achieve an in-flight shutdown rate of 0.05 shutdowns per 1,000hr or five shutdowns in 100,000hr of operation. The rules are even more stringent for 180min ETOPS flights — an in-flight shutdown rate of 0.02 per 1,000hr. In the history of commercial twinjet operation, there has never been an accident as the result of an airliner's two engines failing due to unrelated causes.

In addition to engine design, improvements have been made to other aircraft systems, including electrical power generation, navigation and communication systems, monitoring devices, cargo compartment fire suppression and cabin pressurization.

In designing the 777, Boeing reviewed in-service experience with the 767 and 757 and looked at the reason behind every shutdown

and diversion. On an ETOPS flight, the integrity and reliability of aircraft systems, like electrical generators, becomes especially vital. Boeing incorporated an extra 300 refinements and system changes to ensure adequate redundancy in systems like the auxiliary power unit and electrical power. The engine makers added more than 160 refinements to their engine systems to ensure the 777 met ETOPS standards. The changes were also meant to reduce false alarms — like warnings of an engine fire or low oil pressure — which result in an engine shutdown and diversion to an alternate airport.

But the challenge for Boeing was to demonstrate to the Federal Aviation Administration that the 777 would be ready to fly ETOPS flights from its first day in service, a remarkable first for an all-new aircraft using new engines.

Systems Lab

Meeting the ambitious goal of building a service-ready jetliner approved for 180min ETOPS flying required unprecedented testing. That is why the aircraft's systems began 'flying' almost a year before the 777's first flight. The site of this testing wasn't an airport though but rather the new Integrated Aircraft Systems Laboratory, a three-storey, $360 million centre also known as 'Airplane Zero'.

The facility, located near Boeing Field south of Seattle, is home to 53 labs, including four integration labs, where aircraft components were tested individually and then together as they would be working on the actual aircraft.

Boeing pilots and other members of the flight test team flew hundreds of 'flights' in the new lab, enabling design staff to uncover and correct potential problems not usually caught until the flight tests. Prior to the creation of the lab, avionics, engine and flight controls and the mechanical, electrical and hydraulic systems got their first integrated workout during ground-testing of an aircraft. Free from the usual constraints of weather and air traffic control, the lab is capable of doing testing at about twice the rate of an actual aircraft.

The facility's Systems Integration Laboratory was used to operate electrical and

avionics systems together for the first time as if they were flying. After being tested individually, more than 100 line replaceable units were connected by production wiring and the 777 electrical power generation and distribution systems for testing as an integrated system.

The 777's flight control system, including its fly-by-wire technology and parts of the electrical and hydraulic systems, were tested together on the Flight Controls Test Rig, also known as the 'iron bird'. Signals sent electronically from the rig's flightdeck moved the control surfaces — rudder, elevator,

ailerons, flaperons (which work both as flaps and high-speed ailerons) and spoilers all held in place by a large steel framework. Two flightdeck simulators were used in the cockpit design, development of crew procedures and the early training of Boeing pilots. One simulator had a visual system, allowing Boeing pilots to 'fly' the initial series of test flights before the actual first flight.

Boeing even had a lab to test the cabin fixtures, including the sophisticated new entertainment system for passengers. Called the Passenger Cabin Engineering Lab (PCEL), it was a partial cabin mock-up complete with seats, overhead bins and the seatback video system.

The testing went on 24hr a day, seven days a week, to iron out the bugs before the first flight. In all, various 777 systems underwent 6,122hr of tests. The 777 was the first user of the lab that will be used in the development of other Boeing aircraft.

Orders and Production
The Boeing factory in Everett, Washington — already the world's largest building by

volume and home to the wide-body production of 767s and 747s — got even bigger to make room for the 777 production line.

The expansion, which cost $1.5 billion, enlarged the assembly building by 50% to cover 98.36 acres. The project took more steel than used to build New York's Empire State Building and enough concrete to construct 44 miles of four-lane motorway. Behind the six cavernous hangar doors — each 87ft high and 300ft wide — are two 747 production lines, one 767 line, one 777 line and another assembly bay which could be used for either the 777 or another 747 line.

The 777 has about 132,500 unique engineered parts, more than three million parts in total when rivets, bolts and other fasteners are included. These parts and subassemblies arrive at the factory from hundreds of suppliers around the globe — outboard flaps and radome from Italy; dorsal fin and wingtip assembly from Brazil; the rudders and elevators from Australia and the landing gear from Canada and France. The 777 represents the greatest level of international participation of any Boeing aircraft. The largest overseas participants are the Japanese airframe manufacturers which signed on as risk-sharing programme partners in the spring of 1991. Mitsubishi, Kawasaki and Fuji heavy industries helped design and build about 20% of the airframe structure. The large wing centre section, for example, is made by Fuji Heavy Industries. It is shipped in a container about the size of a small house and arrives by boat at the port of Tacoma. From there it is moved by barge and then train up one of the steepest railway gradients in the USA to get to the factory.

In January 1993, workers in Everett loaded a 105ft-long wing spar into an automated spar assembly tool, a new device that automatically drills, measures and installs more than 5,000 fasteners into the structure. The event marked the start of major assembly on the first 777. Over the ensuing months, the first 777 took shape on the factory floor as thousands of pieces came together. The first major body sections arrived from Japan, the nose and engine struts from Wichita. In July, the aft fuselage section was assembled in an

inverted position and then rotated upright in a 190,000lb turning fixture. This 14,000lb section of the aircraft houses the aft cargo hold and economy section of the cabin. Later that month, the first assembled wing structure was completed. The left wing was gingerly lifted out of a rig where it had been fabricated. Work then continued on the wing, such as sealing its innards to hold fuel, in preparation for its mating with the centre fuselage section and right wing.

By September 1993, the forward portions of the aircraft, known as Sections 41 and 43, had been joined. Assembly continued on the interior structure and workers began installing the passenger doors. A month later, the wings were joined to the centre section of the aircraft body.

The large aircraft sections entered final body join in December, and for the first time, the 777 resembled an entire aircraft, complete with a tail. Because there had been no mock-up, this was the first sense workers got of how big the aircraft truly was. In January 1994, the 777 was moved on its own landing gear to final assembly, the last position before leaving the factory. This is where the aircraft get their engines. Electrical power was turned on for the first time to test aircraft systems.

The development of the 777 took place against a troubled backdrop. A worldwide recession had crippled the world's airlines and claimed such auspicious names as Pan Am and Eastern. The economic slowdown came just as aircraft manufacturers delivered a record number of aircraft, all ordered during the boom years of the late 1980s. This excess capacity led to record losses. Between 1990 and 1991, orders dropped precipitously and the number of parked aircraft doubled from 500 to 1,000. Boeing could not escape the impact. From 1991 to 1994, the aircraft maker chopped production rates by almost half and cut its workforce by thousands as orders dried up.

Still, Boeing was taking orders for the 777 at an encouraging pace. In 1992, Cathay Pacific Airways announced orders for 11 777s and options for a further 11; Emirates said it would take seven 777s and options for an additional seven. Three of Emirates' 777s are

The 777 has enjoyed a worldwide appeal. Boeing boasts that the aircraft has captured 75% of its market since the programme was launched in October, 1990. By the end of 1996, 45 777s had been delivered to nine airlines around the world. *Emirates*

the base model and the balance of orders and options are for the longer-range version. The year ended with the 15 December order from International Lease Finance Corp (ILFC) for six longer-range 777s and options for two others, followed three days later with the announcement from China Southern Airlines that it was ordering six 777s.

The following year marked a turnaround as airlines boosted load factors, cut costs and restructured to return to profitability. The 777 order book continued to grow. Continental Airlines ordered five longer-range 777s and options for five more on 12 May 1993, making it the second US carrier to take the jet. The aircraft's popularity in Asia was

further confirmed in June when Japan Air System ordered seven 777s. Gulf Air, the flag carrier of Abu Dhabi, Bahrain, Oman and Qatar ordered six of the longer-range wide-bodies. But after some analysis of its fleet requirements, the carrier decided the 777s would add too much capacity and cancelled the order. Completing 1993 was Transbrasil's 15 December order for three initial-model 777s, an order it too would later cancel, and Korean Air's order for eight longer-range 777s and options for an extra eight.

By 1994, the 777's four-year gestation was nearly over but the jet still faced daunting milestones: roll-out was in April 1994, first flight that June. And then was to come a year of testing to earn type certification and approval for 180min ETOPS in time for delivery to United Airlines, which was making plans for the new equipment in its worldwide schedule.

It was to be a very busy year.

Key Programme Dates	
Programme Launch:.	29 October 1990
Start of major assembly:	21 January 1993
Ceremonial rollout:	9 April 1994
First flight:	12 June 1994
FAA/JAA type certification:	19 April 1995
First delivery:	15 May 1995
FAA ETOPS approval:	30 May 1995
First revenue flight:	7 June 1995

2. Nose To Tail

The technological advancements of the 777 — and the philosophy behind them — were in part shaped by Boeing's earlier work on an airliner that never got off the drawing board.

That aircraft was the 7J7 and it was designed in the mid-1980s to incorporate a number of revolutionary developments. The plans called for an aircraft powered by two high bypass engines driving propfans, built from new structural materials and featuring improved avionics and a new wing design — advances that in many ways were a precursor of the 777.

But during the 7J7 development at least one airline criticized Boeing for putting technology on the aircraft without considering whether the high-tech advances offered any benefits. It was an important message for the aircraft maker to hear and one that would later influence the 777. When it came time to design the 777, technology was included only if it improved the aircraft's economics, reliability or maintainability.

As a result, the 777 is a mix of tried and trusted technology honed over decades of building jets and the latest in new technology developed in the decade since Boeing's last all-new jet.

Fly-by-Wire

One of the biggest advances on the 777 is its fly-by-wire (FBW) flight control system. Rival Airbus Industrie has long been using FBW on its jets, starting with the A320 in 1987. The 777 however marks the first time that it has been used on a Boeing aircraft.

Boeing had explored the possible use of a digital fly-by-wire system and even tested sidestick controllers for its 7J7 project. The 7J7 never got off the ground but the research into fly-by-wire flight control laid the foundation for the 777 system and gave Boeing a good understanding of the benefits of the technology. In a conventional aircraft, cables running from the cockpit controls connect with actuators in the wings and tail which move the elevators, rudder, ailerons, flaps and slats. In a fly-by-wire jet, the pilot's commands — made through the control wheel and rudder pedals — are converted to electrical signals and transmitted through computers and electrical wires to the actuators.

The big advantage of a FBW system are the flight computers which refine pilot commands to improve handling and provide protection against violent manoeuvring. By eliminating the long cable runs, pulleys and

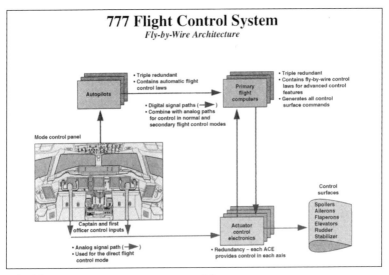

777 Flight Control System
Fly-by-Wire Architecture

Autopilots
- Triple redundant
- Contains automatic flight control laws

Primary flight computers
- Triple redundant
- Contains fly-by-wire control laws for advanced control features
- Generates all control surface commands

- Digital signal paths (———►)
- Combine with analog paths for control in normal and secondary flight control modes

Mode control panel

Captain and first officer control inputs

- Analog signal path (———►)
- Used for the direct flight control mode

Actuator control electronics
- Redundancy – each ACE provides control in each axis

Control surfaces
- Spoilers
- Ailerons
- Flaperons
- Elevators
- Rudder
- Stabilizer

Below left:
The built-in protections of the fly-by-wire system not only improve safety but because of the system's fast response, the vertical fin and horizontal stabilizer are smaller than those on a conventionally controlled aircraft.
Boeing

Below:
Reverse thrust is just coming on as this Japan Airlines 777 slows on the runway. The control laws and features of the new fly-by-wire system were incorporated into a modified 757 and test flown in the summer of 1992.
Boeing

Above:
The operation of the fly-by-wire system.
Boeing

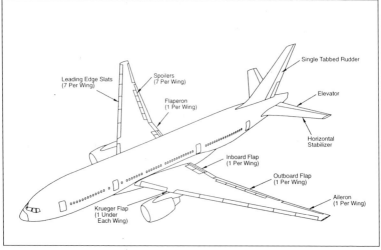

Above:
The flight controls. *Boeing*

Below:
The high-lift devices on the 777. *Boeing*

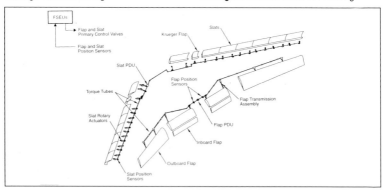

brackets, FBW saves weight and reduces the work required to maintain the complicated rigging for the control cables.

A better description of the system might be fly-through-computer. When the pilot moves the control column, position transducers convert the movement to analogue electrical signals which go to actuator control electronic units (ACEs). These units change the signals to digital format and send them to the three primary flight computers (PFCs) which calculate the proper commands for roll, pitch and yaw based on the built-in logic of the system and the protection against potentially dangerous manoeuvres. Within each PFC are three separate microprocessors, each performing independent calculations. Each PFC can operate safely with only two lanes. The digital command signals return to the ACEs where they are converted back to analogue format and sent to the actuators to move the control surfaces.

Because there are no direct links between the controls and the control columns, actuators are used to artificially create control forces to provide feedback for the pilots. The conventional cockpit controls are similar to those on earlier Boeing models, an intentional move by designers to ease the transition for new pilots. Those who fly the 777 say the control forces are lighter than on other Boeing wide-bodies and describe the handling as more precise.

The control logic of Boeing's FBW system is governed by speed stability — the aircraft is trimmed to a particular speed and any deviation from that speed will cause a change in pitch to recapture it. Otherwise, trimming is only required to change airspeed. The system automatically retrims the aircraft to compensate for pitch changes that occur when flaps, spoilers and gear are extended or retracted or the thrust settings are changed.

The FBW system includes a number of built-in protections to prevent the aircraft from being banked too steeply or flown too slowly or too fast. These features are meant to deter pilot actions but unlike the absolute protections of the Airbus system, Boeing's safeguards can be overridden, leaving the final authority with the flightcrew.

For example, in a turn greater than 35° bank, bank angle protection requires the pilot to use additional force on the control column to maintain altitude and bank angle. These cues alert the pilot that he or she risks putting the aircraft outside its normal operating envelope. But in keeping with

Boeing's philosophy, the pilot can override the system by exerting greater force. In more gentle turns — no more than 30° — a feature called 'turn compensation' automatically applies back pressure and trims to maintain constant altitude.

If the aircraft is flown too slowly or too fast, the control forces increase substantially and the system will not allow the pilot to trim below a minimum safe speed or above the maximum operating speed. Another feature called 'thrust asymmetry compensation' helps the pilots control the aircraft during an engine failure. If the thrust of the two engines differs by more than 10%, rudder is automatically applied to counter the resulting yaw. This feature becomes active at about 80kt. A separate function, called 'gust

Below:
The single-slotted outboard flaps and inboard, double-slotted flaps are well displayed as this All Nippon 777 takes to the sky. The aircraft has a feature called flap load relief. If the 777 accelerates past the safe flap extension speed, the flaps will retract and then redeploy as the jet slows again. Likewise, if the flaps are selected and the aircraft is going too fast, the devices will not lower until the aircraft slows to the proper speed. *Boeing*

suppression', senses wind gusts on the tail and applies rudder to oppose it. This improves the ride for passengers by minimizing uncomfortable yawing movement.

Roll control is through low-speed ailerons, inboard flaperons and spoilers. The ailerons on the outboard section of the trailing edge move up 33° and down 19° to provide improved roll control at lower speeds. They are locked out at higher speeds, generally when flaps are up, and the flaperons used for roll control. In the air, spoiler panels on each wing can operate independently to improve roll control or together to slow the aircraft or speed descent. After landing, the panels automatically deploy on wheel spin-up to spoil lift and put the aircraft weight on the wheels for better braking.

The elevators are used for initial pitch attitude, and the stabilizer moves to trim the aircraft. When approaching a stall, the flight computers will command the elevator to pitch the nose down. Likewise, if the aircraft is going too fast, the nose will pitch up. During the flare, the flight computers command a pitch down to simulate the natural attitude of the aircraft in ground effect. The elevators move 33° up and 27° down.

The FBW system has a normal mode and two back-ups to ensure redundancy. The first back-up (secondary mode) occurs if the system loses sensor data and operates the same as normal mode except for the loss of the autopilot and some envelope protection functions. The second back-up (direct mode) is used if sensor data degrades further or failures render the first two modes unreliable. In this case, the primary flight computers are bypassed and pilot commands go directly to actuator control electronics to move the flight controls. Control in this mode remains excellent and the aircraft handles much like the Boeing 767.

In the unlikely event that all else fails, the pilots can still land the 777 using mechanical linkages. A spoiler on each wing and the stabilizer pitch trim are cable-driven, allowing rudimentary pitch and roll control.

Credit for the 777's good take-off and landing performance goes to the system of flaps and slats which change the profile of the wing to provide extra lift at lower airspeeds. A double-slotted flap is located on the inboard trailing edge of each wing between the fuselage and engine and a larger, single-slotted flap is positioned outboard. On the leading edge of each wing are seven slats and one Krueger flap to further assist low-speed flight.

The take-off flap settings are 5°, 15° and 20°; landing settings are 25° and 30°. When the flaps extend, the ailerons and flaperons also move down to increase lift while still providing roll control. The uniquely designed flaperons droop 34° to become a slotted flap. The slats and flaps are moved by hydraulics but can also be deployed and retracted by back-up electrical motors.

Flightdeck
Despite the advances of the FBW system, Boeing purposely stuck to a traditional flightdeck design similar in appearance to the 747-400 while sharing the twin-engined systems controls of the 757 and 767.

It is a design honed by nearly 700 industry and airline pilots who logged more than 5,800hr in the 777 simulator. Their suggestions led to a clean, uncluttered flightdeck and influenced such things as the use of larger, easier to read lettering on the instrument panels and even the location of the cup holders.

First stop for new 777 pilots is the simulator. Here a flight crew is at work in a CAE 777 simulator. It takes a minimum of 11 days before a pilot of a 767 or a 747-400 can progress to the 777. *CAE*

The 777's avionics undergoing testing by Honeywell engineers. *Honeywell*

Six large displays across the instrument panel resemble the cathode ray tubes used on the 747-400 but in fact are more advanced liquid crystal displays. Compared to displays found in the first 'glass cockpits', these so-called 'flat panel displays' save space, weight and power and generate less heat, eliminating the need for complex air conditioning ducting. The new displays, each 8in by 8in, are also easier to read in a variety of lighting conditions, especially direct sunlight. And in a testament to the reliability of the new technology, even the three standby instruments for attitude, altitude and airspeed are flat panel displays rather than the traditional analogue dials.

In front of each pilot are two displays. The outboard screen is typically used for primary flight information such as attitude, airspeed, altitude, vertical speed and heading. The inboard screen shows navigation data. A moving map display highlights waypoints along the route in ranges from 10nm to 640nm. Returns from the weather radar can be overlaid the map display.

The other two displays are set one above the other in the centre panel. The top display is used for the engine indication and crew alerting system (EICAS) and shows primary engine instrumentation, position of flaps and landing gear and a variety of other information, including warning, caution and advisory messages. Below that is a multi-function display where pilots can call up synoptic diagrams showing the status of flight controls, landing gear, doors and the fuel, hydraulic, electrical and environmental

control systems. The actual controls for the aircraft systems are on the overhead panel. The 777 flightdeck incorporates a number of features, including:

• An improved data link to receive weather reports, airline messages and air traffic control instructions.

• Full-time operation of all three autopilot channels whenever the autopilot mode is selected by the pilots. Unlike the Airbus design, the control columns and throttles move to provide the pilots visual cues of the autopilot and autothrottle operation.

• A satellite communications system and global positioning system (GPS) installed as basic equipment. The SATCOM system uses a network of satellites to relay voice and data communications to ground stations when out of VHF range. It is unaffected by the atmospheric disturbances which can make the high frequency radios now in use undecipherable. GPS gives greater accuracy in navigation and is used by the flight management computer in combination with other navigational equipment to precisely determine the 777's position. The aircraft is also equipped with the usual complement of VHF and HF communication radios; navigation radios such as VOR, DME, ILS; radio altimeters; traffic alert and collision avoidance systems and ground proximity warning systems.

• An engine failure alert to help the pilots recognize and confirm an engine failure. On take-off, if an engine is not supplying the thrust commanded by the pilot or suffers a complete failure, an automated voice will call out 'Engine Fail', the master warning light will illuminate and the message 'ENG FAIL' will appear on primary flight display.

• Electronic checklists. Normal and non-normal checklists can be called up on the multi-function display. These checklists are an electronic version of the checks outlined in the aircraft's operations manual. The avionics system senses the position of many switches, controls and other data and automatically indicates completed items.

• Cursor control devices. The two devices, located on either side of the centre console

just ahead of the throttles, are used by the pilots to select items on the multi-function display and on the two optional side displays located on the outboard sides of the cockpit. The pilots control checklists and other functions by moving their finger on the touch-sensitive screens of the cursor devices, working it much like the mouse on a personal computer.

The electronic brain of the 777 is an advanced avionics system that runs the cockpit displays and provides the pilots with information on maintenance faults, navigation, status of aircraft systems and handles key functions including the flight management system, thrust and communications.

Made by Honeywell, it is known as the 'aircraft information management system', or AIMS for short. Honeywell boasts that the revolutionary avionics has given the 777 the best 'brains' in the business. Designing this system was the largest single research and development project in Honeywell's 110-year history.

The heart of AIMS is a cabinet in the main equipment centre — the 777 has two identical AIMS cabinets for redundancy — that contains the central processing and hardware for these functions. In other aircraft, each of these functions is done in separate line replaceable units (LRU), resulting in considerable duplication of hardware and software common to all the units.

What makes AIMS unique is that it combines these tasks in a single cabinet so they can share the same power supply, processor, memory systems, operating system, utility software, input/output ports and built-in test equipment. This sharing is made possible by advances in two areas. The first is robust software partitioning which prevents a glitch in one software from contaminating other software. Application-specific integrated circuits (ASICs) enable more system functions to run in a single processor channel.

The result, according to Honeywell, is a significant saving in cost and weight as well as much better reliability and easier maintenance. Both AIMS and flat panel technology are sophisticated advances that Honeywell expects will be used in upgrades of military aircraft, in the Space Shuttle and will become the new standard for airliners of

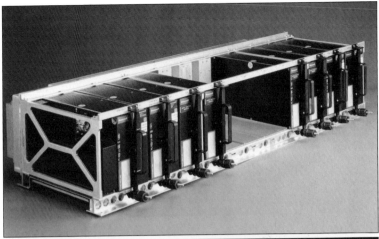

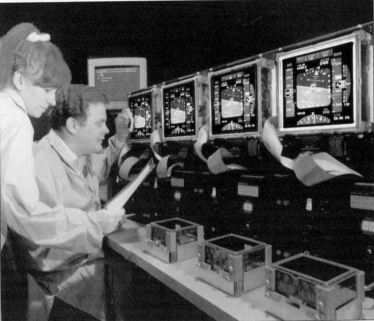

the future.

Among AIMS' vital functions is the flight management system which assists the pilots with navigation and flight planning and calculates the most economical profiles for climbs, descents and cruise. The flight management computer has a navigation database that contains navaid locations, waypoints, departure and arrival procedures and company flight plans. The computer also automatically tunes navaids throughout the flight. On the centre console are three, full-colour multipurpose control display units, or CDUs, used by the pilots to programme the flight management computer.

Another important AIMS function is the central maintenance computer system. An upgrade of the system installed on the 747-400, the maintenance computer collects detailed data on about 87 aircraft systems and components such as air conditioning, electrical, fire protection, brakes and hydraulics. At the end of a flight, a line mechanic uses the computer to isolate faults that may have occurred on the last leg. Easier trouble-shooting speeds repairs and reduces so-called 'shotgun' maintenance. This has meant fewer frustrating flight delays and cancellations that result when mechanics are unable to pinpoint a problem. Maintenance crews access the system through a computer terminal behind the first officer's seat on the flightdeck. They can also plug in portable computer terminals and access the system from links in the nosewheel well, main equipment centre, a spot behind the mainwheel well and in the area of the stabilizer.

Another function called the 'airplane condition monitoring system' tracks the performance of the engines and aircraft systems, giving the airline a record for maintenance, trouble-shooting and following trends.

The computers in AIMS and the fly-by-wire system 'talk' to one another through a new two-way databus called ARINC 629. It permits aircraft systems and their computers to communicate through a common wire path instead of through separate one-way connections.

There are 11 ARINC 629 pathways on the 777.

Honeywell also supplies an advanced unit called ADIRS which combines the functions of air data sensing and inertial reference. At the heart of the unit are six accelerometers and six tiny, ring-laser gyros, which could fit in the

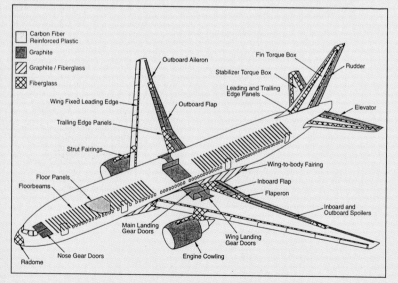

Carbon Fiber Reinforced Plastic
Graphite
Graphite / Fiberglass
Fiberglass

Outboard Aileron
Fin Torque Box
Rudder
Stabilizer Torque Box
Leading and Trailing Edge Panels
Wing Fixed Leading Edge
Outboard Flap
Elevator
Trailing Edge Panels
Strut Fairings
Wing-to-body Fairing
Floor Panels
Inboard Flap
Floorbeams
Flaperon
Inboard and Outboard Spoilers
Main Landing Gear Doors
Wing Landing Gear Doors
Nose Gear Doors
Engine Cowling
Radome

Below left:
The aircraft's composite structure. Boeing

Right:
A total of 9% of the 777's structural weight is made from composites, including most of the tail section. Author

palm of a hand. Lasers are beamed in opposite directions through the triangular gyros, reflected off mirrors in each corner. When the aircraft attitude changes, the light beams are minutely affected. A computer detects and measures the differences among several gyros to determine even the slightest change in the aircraft's position. Innovative fibre optic gyros provide the back-up sensors.

New Materials

A number of advanced composite materials and new alloys are used throughout the 777. In the upper wing skin and stringers, an improved aluminium alloy known as 7055-T77 is used for greater strength against the compression, or bending loads, and improved resistance against corrosion and fatigue. The new alloy 2524-T3 was developed for the fuselage skin and the aft pressure bulkhead. It has better fracture toughness than the alloy 2024-T3 used in the past. Another alloy called 7150-T77 is used in the stringers along the top and bottom of the fuselage structure to support the skin and the seat tracks.

Composites are also used to a greater extent than ever before on a Boeing commercial jet. These materials total about 9% of the structural weight of the 777, compared to about 3% on previous Boeing jets. Boeing has been using the material on secondary components, like flaps and rudders, since 1982. But the 777 marks the first time that composites have been used on major load-carrying structures. The vertical and horizontal stabilizer main torque boxes on the aircraft are made from a carbon fibre reinforced plastic material. These tough, lightweight materials made from plastic, carbon fibres and graphite-epoxy resin are also used on engine cowlings, flight control surfaces, floor beams, landing gear doors and fairings.

Above:
The unique six-wheel landing gear is the largest installed on a commercial jet. The design spreads the weight of the aircraft and eliminates the need for a third set of wheels under the fuselage. *Author*

Above right:
Actuators tilt the main gear trucks about 13° up when extended for landing and after take-off and 5° down during retraction for stowage in the wheel wells. *Boeing*

Hydraulics

The hydraulic systems are the muscles that operate the moving parts of the aircraft. The 777 has three independent 3,000psi systems providing hydraulic power to operate such functions as the primary flight controls, high-lift devices and landing gear. A combination of pneumatic, engine-driven and electrical pumps pressurize the systems, sending virtually incompressible hydraulic fluid along tubes to move aircraft components in response to actions by the pilots, like lowering the flaps or steering the nosewheel. All three systems supply pressure to the primary flight controls, ensuring the 777 can be controlled with the loss of any of the two systems. In addition, the left system also powers the left thrust reverser. The right system supplies the right thrust reverser and the normal main gear brakes. The centre system provides hydraulic pressure to the alternate main gear brakes, nose and main gear steering, landing gear extension and retraction, leading edge slats and trailing edge flaps. The components for the left and right systems are near the engine struts and those for the centre system are in the area of the main landing gear wheels. The tubing for the individual systems is routed to ensure that a catastrophic structural or engine failure does not cause a pressure loss in all three systems. For example, only one hydraulic system has tubing within an engine strut and nacelle. In the wings, one system is forward of the rear spar and two systems are behind it and only two systems go to the end of the wings.

The left and right systems each have an engine-driven pump (EDP) as a primary pump that operates continuously and an alternating current electrical pump (ACMP) which operates only to boost flow when there is a heavy demand on the system.

The centre system has two primary

electrical pumps and two air-driven pumps
(ADPs) that operate as demand pumps
powered by compressed air from the aircraft's
pneumatic system. This combination of
pumps gives the centre system more capacity
than the other two. The centre system also
has a ram air turbine (RAT) pump for an
emergency source of hydraulic pressure for
the primary flight controls. The RAT is a small
propeller, 3.5ft in diameter, that is spun by
the airstream to turn a hydraulic pump and
electric generator. Located in the wing-to-
body fairing behind the right wheel well, it
automatically extends when there is a loss of
hydraulic pressure, a loss of electrical power
to the ac buses or a loss of rpm from both
engines. Because of the increased demand of
the 777's flight control system, the RAT on
this aircraft is larger than those on the 757
and 767.

Electrics

The 777's electrical power system is similar to
the configuration found on the smaller twins,
the 757 and 767, but has additional

generating capacity to handle the heavier
consumption of the cabin entertainment
system and fly-by-wire system.

Two integrated drive generators (IDG), one
on each engine gearbox, are the prime source
of power. Each generator supplies up to
120kVA — enough to power up to 40
average homes — compared to 90kVA on
the 767 and 747-400. Since the engine speed
varies during flight, within each IDG is a
constant speed drive which keeps the
generator speed constant during the flight.

There is also a back-up generator on each
engine gearbox, a new feature of the 777 for
extra redundancy for ETOPS flights. These
variable-speed, variable-frequency generators
can each supply up to 20kVA of ac power. A
convertor changes the variable frequency
power to constant frequency power. On the
same shaft as the back-up generator are two
permanent magnet generators on each
engine which power the fly-by-wire system.
In case of a failure, the FBW system can draw
from other sources including the 28V dc
buses.

Top:
This dramatic shot shows off a design feature of the 777 that is a first for Boeing jetliners — a perfectly round fuselage. The fuselages of other jets had two different cross-sections faired together in the middle. *John M. Dibbs*

Above:
At 19ft 3in, the 777's fuselage is wider than any other jetliner except for its larger sibling, the 747. *United Airlines*

Top:
Many operators have installed high-tech passenger entertainment systems on their 777s, like this one on an Emirates 777. Travellers have a wide choice of video and audio channels or can play a video game or shop for duty-free items. *Emirates*

Above:
Flight attendants use touch-screen computers to select boarding music and adjust cabin temperature, check the status of water, food and drink inventories and whether doors are properly closed. *United Airlines*

A third 120kVA generator is on the Allied Signal Engines 331-500 auxiliary power unit (APU) located in the tail cone. The APU supplies both electricity for aircraft systems and pneumatic power for air conditioning and engine starts. This allows independent operation on the ground and emergency back-up in the air. The APU itself was subjected to an unprecedented 20,000hr of testing and 22,000 starts before entering operation, 900 of those starts in Alaska after being cold-soaked to temperatures typical of high altitude flight. The power unit is equipped with both an electric and air turbine starter and uses electric heat to warm the gearbox and bearing assembly to ensure successful cold starts. The electrical power system normally operates as two independent left and right power channels, each with a main ac bus and powered by the IDG on their respective engine. The APU generator and external power sources also provide ac power for either main bus. Five 120A transformer rectifier units make 28V dc power from ac power.

If all ac power is lost in flight, the main battery initially supplies the dc loads directly and the ac loads through the static inverter. Less than a minute after ac power loss, the ram air turbine will automatically deploy to supply up to 7.5kVA from its electric generator to the dc and ac standby systems. When parked at the gate, the 777 can be connected to ground power using two receptacles rated for 90kVA of ac power located near the nose.

An electrical load management system handles the distribution as well as monitoring of electrical power throughout the aircraft. It controls such tasks as electric load shedding, standby power, galley power, and APU starting. When an electrical bus switches from one power source to another, two sources will momentarily supply the bus to ensure no break in power.

Landing Gear

The 777 stands on a uniquely arranged landing gear that is the largest ever installed on a commercial jet. Each of the two main gear legs has three axles and six wheels rather than the conventional four-wheel units.

It is an arrangement similar to that found on a Russian jetliner, the Tu-154, but the first time it has been used on a US design. With 12 wheels altogether, the design of the 777's main gear provides better weight distribution on runways and taxiways and avoids the need for an extra two-wheel unit under the fuselage. The main landing gear stand about 14ft tall, providing clearance for the huge engine intakes.

Two tillers on either side of the cockpit move the nosewheel 70° in each direction for taxiing. To assist steering, the aft axles on the main gear turn up to 8° in either direction to reduce the turning radius and tyre scrubbing. It is activated automatically whenever the nosewheel turns more than 13°.

Carbon brakes on each of the main wheels provide the stopping power for the 777 and a digital unit controls the anti-skid and autobrake systems. The brakes are applied by toe pedals or automatically by the autobrake during landing roll-out. Before landing, the pilots arm the autobrake system and select one of five deceleration rates. A separate rejected take-off setting, selected before take-off, automatically applies maximum braking if the take-off roll is aborted. Brake temperatures and tyre pressures for each individual wheel can be monitored by the pilots on the cockpit EICAS display. At low speeds, braking is alternated between four of the six brakes on each truck to reduce brake wear. One feature sure to be popular with ground crews are lights on the nose gear to indicate when the brakes and the parking brake are applied.

Pressure from the centre hydraulic system raises and lowers the gear. If hydraulic pressure is lost, an alternate gear extension system unlocks the landing gear and the gear doors, allowing the wheels to drop into position by their own weight.

Fuel

The 777's fuel load is stored in the thick wings and the centre section of the fuselage. The 777-200 has three tanks with a total capacity of 31,000gal of fuel: two main tanks in the body of the wing, which each hold 9,300gal; and a 12,400gal centre tank. The centre tank is actually in two sections, one in

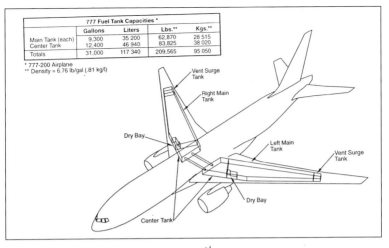

777 Fuel Tank Capacities *				
	Gallons	Liters	Lbs.**	Kgs.**
Main Tank (each)	9,300	35 200	62,870	28 515
Center Tank	12,400	46 940	83,825	38 020
Totals	31,000	117 340	209,565	95 050

* 777-200 Airplane
** Density = 6.76 lb/gal (.81 kg/l)

Above:
The fuel system. *Boeing*

each wing inboard of the engine, divided by a dry bay where it passes through the fuselage. The two sections are connected by two tubes to keep the fuel loads balanced. On both the 777-200IGW and the 777-300, the centre tank runs through the fuselage and fills this unused space. This raises the centre tank's capacity to 26,100gal and the total fuel capacity of both models to 45,220gal.

The left and right tanks are vented through channels in the wing to surge tanks on the outboard section of the wings to keep the tanks near ambient pressure during flight. The surge tanks also hold the fuel that may flow out from the main tanks during a turn or if the tanks are overfilled.

The tanks are filled through a fuelling point on the leading edge of the left wing. Fuel quantity is measured in unusual fashion by 52 ultrasonic sensors that detect the height and density of fuel in each tank. A processor then calculates the total weight of fuel onboard. Each tank has two ac-powered pumps, each capable of 5,255gal/hr. The 777-300 has higher capacity pumps to feed the increased demand of its higher thrust engines. At the start of a flight, when the tanks are full, all fuel pumps are normally turned on. Fuel in the centre tank is used first because the two override/jettison pumps in this tank have a higher output pressure than the main tank pumps. When the centre tank

gets low, two boost pumps in each main tank automatically begin to feed the engines. The override/jettison pumps are turned off by the flight crew and the remaining fuel in the centre tank is then automatically transferred to the main tanks by a scavenge pump.

If a bird strike or passenger illness requires an unplanned landing, fuel can be dumped overboard through a nozzle on the trailing edge of each wing to avoid an overweight landing. The jettison system is turned on by the pilots and automatically stops pumping fuel overboard when it reaches the maximum landing weight or an amount manually selected by the pilots.

Cabin
The bigger engines and the high-tech wizardry would count for little if the passengers were uncomfortable. Boeing spent a lot of time working on the cabin, using both design and new technology to impress travellers. The cabin is strikingly spacious, thanks in part to its width — at 19ft 3in, the 777's fuselage is wider than any other jetliner except for its larger sibling, the 747. Design features also complement the spacious feel.

43

Above:
Next stop, the paint shop. *Boeing*

Right:
A thorough scrubbing with soap, water and solvents removes traces of dirt, grease and the green primer that protects the airframe during assembly. Windows and other unpainted areas get a protective spray before being covered with paper and tape. *Boeing*

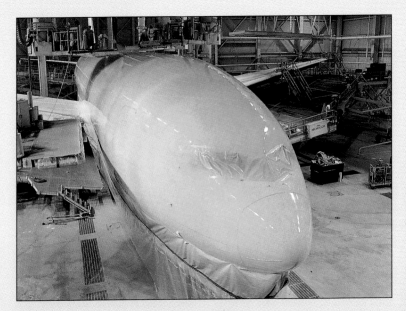

Above:
The aircraft first gets a coat of yellow primer, followed by a white coat which dries for an hour and then is cured for four more hours at 120° F. *Boeing*

Below:
Templates and stencils are used to transfer the airline's logos on to the aircraft. Four days in the paint shop transforms plain-looking aircraft into brightly coloured flying billboards. *Boeing*

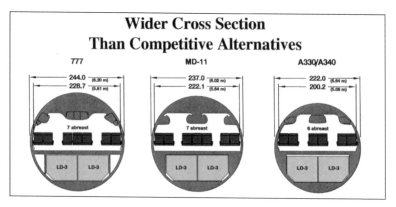

Wider Cross Section Than Competitive Alternatives

777

244.0 (6.20 m)
228.7 (5.81 m)

7 abreast

LD-3 | LD-3

MD-11

237.0 (6.02 m)
222.1 (5.64 m)

7 abreast

LD-3 | LD-3

A330/A340

222.0 (5.64 m)
200.2 (5.09 m)

6 abreast

LD-3 | LD-3

Indirect lighting and bigger windows make the cabin brighter. The seats are wider and straighter cabin walls give more shoulder room for passengers sitting in window seats. The large, drop-down overhead stowage bins recess neatly out of the way into the high sculpted ceilings to give 6ft, 4in of headroom under the bins. The two-aisle cabin can be configured six seats abreast in first class, six or eight abreast in business class and nine or 10 abreast in economy.

A taste of the aircraft's advanced electronics has found its way back into the cabin in the form of a high-tech entertainment system some airlines are installing in their 777s. Video screens are built into the seat backs and a handset works as a credit card reader, telephone and controller for the audio and video functions. Passengers have their pick of up to 15 channels of video selections and 24 channels of CD-quality sound. The interactive video system offers endless possibilities for travellers to pass the time playing a video game or watching a map showing the aircraft's current position. On some airlines, passengers are able to connect

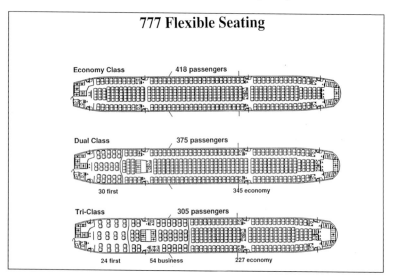

777 Flexible Seating

Economy Class   418 passengers

Dual Class   375 passengers

30 first   345 economy

Tri-Class   305 passengers

24 first   54 business   227 economy

laptop computers and modems to telephones and send e-mail and faxes. Soon travellers will be able to shop for duty-free items from their seat using a video catalogue. It's a far cry from the days when all a passenger had was two buttons, one to turn on a reading light and another to call the flight attendant.

So-called 'flex zones' have been designed into the cabin to give airlines the flexibility to change cabin configuration and the seating arrangements, like making the business section larger. The plumbing and electrical fixtures in the cabin are built so the lavatories and galleys can be moved in one-inch increments within these zones. The overhead storage compartments can be quickly removed without disturbing ceiling panels or the air conditioning ducts. All the seat tracks within these zones are made from titanium to withstand corrosion from the inevitable leaks and spills. As a result of this flexibility, a 777 cabin can be reconfigured in as little as 72hr, compared to two or three weeks on other aircraft. Those time savings are significant for an airline like British Airways which redesigns at least one of its classes every 18 months.

The cabin is pressurized by compressed air drawn from the high pressure compressor of each engine, just before the combustion chamber. Although clean and breathable, the air is extremely hot — a by-product of compression is heat — and must first be cooled before it reaches the cabin. The air is routed into air conditioning packs in the aircraft's belly where the wing meets the fuselage. Cold ambient air is drawn through a ram air inlet into the primary and secondary

heat exchangers to cool the hot bleed air before being exhausted overboard. The compressed air passes through the turbine of an air cycle machine which re-expands it for further cooling. From there, the conditioned air enters a manifold near the back of the forward cargo hold. Risers carry the air to the top of the cabin where ducts vent the air into the cabin.

About half the air passes through filters and is recirculated back into the cabin to reduce the draw on the engines. Cabin pressure is controlled by two outflow valves which open and close to change the rate that air leaves the aircraft. The maximum pressure differential — the difference in pressure between the inside and outside of the aircraft — is 8.6psi.

The upgraded air conditioning system provides passengers with fresher air than on many other aircraft thanks to an improved air filter system and better airflow. The cabin is divided into six zones, each with its own computerized temperature controls for better control of heating and cooling. Because of this, gaspers, the familiar air outlets above each seat, are no longer standard.

Below the main deck, hot air from the pneumatic system heats the aft and bulk cargo areas. That, combined with ventilation fans, allows live animals to be transported in the bulk compartment. In the forward part of the aircraft, 'waste' air used to cool equipment is vented to warm the front cargo compartment.

In the event that cabin pressure is lost, the flight crew would don oxygen masks supplied by a high pressure oxygen cylinder beneath the cabin floor in the main equipment centre. In the cabin, masks would automatically drop from overhead stowage compartments when the cabin altitude reaches 13,500ft or could be deployed by the pilots. Chemical oxygen generators would supply the masks during the short time it takes the flight crew to descend to an altitude where supplementary oxygen is no longer required.

In addition to pressurizing and ventilating the cabin, hot bleed engine air is also used to start the APU and engines and is carried by tubing to de-ice the airframe and engine nacelles.

Above:
The 199ft wingspan is the key to the aircraft's good performance. Boeing designed a special wing with a hinge that would allow 22ft of each wing to fold up, reducing the span to 155ft. Most airlines, though, operate the aircraft from wide-body gates and by 1997, there had been no orders for the folding wing. *Boeing*

Below:
Sunset illuminates the sweep of the 777's fuel-efficient, high-speed wing. In the 777X models, the wing will be structurally strengthened, the span increased slightly and the fuel tanks extended into the outer wings for extra capacity. *Boeing*

Water for drinking, sinks, toilets and galleys is stored in two 109gal tanks behind the bulk cargo compartment and is pressurized by the pneumatic system. The so-called 'grey water' that goes down the drains in the galleys and lavatories is dumped overboard through two heated drain masts on the belly of the aircraft. Waste flushed from the lavatories is collected in three tanks near the aft cargo hold which can hold 189gal in total. The holding tanks are emptied by 'honey' trucks after landing. Below 16,000ft, two vacuum blowers create the suction to drain the toilets into the tanks. Above that altitude, the lower outside air pressure is used to provide the suction.

The fuselage cross-section of the 777 is perfectly round, a first for a Boeing jetliner. The circular fuselage makes for not only a spacious cabin but generous cargo holds able to accommodate the standard LD-3 cargo containers. Two main holds, forward and aft, have a total volume of 5,056cu ft, enough to accommodate 32 LD-3 containers. A separate compartment at the back of the aft hold has room for 600cu ft of bulk-loaded cargo. The cargo capacity grows with the stretched 777-300 version to 7,080cu ft of lower hold volume, including the bulk compartment.

Wing Design

In the sleek line of the 777 wing is what Boeing calls 'the most aerodynamically efficient aerofoil ever developed for subsonic commercial aviation'.

It started with a request from the airlines. They wanted the 777 to fly faster than the 767, which cruises at Mach 0.80. That speed is fine for short to medium distance routes for which the 767 was originally designed. But the slower speed prolongs longer flights, like those envisaged for the 777.

The result is a new, supercritical aerofoil design that Boeing will probably use in different sizes for the next 20 years. A refinement of the efficient wing designs introduced on the 757 and 767, the 777 wing creates lift across more of its upper surface, farther back towards the trailing edge. The point where the smooth airflow across the top of a wing becomes turbulent is called the 'transition point'. The farther back the transition point, the more efficient the wing. On the 777 wing, this transition occurs at about 80% of the chord, compared to 60% for traditional designs. The engines also sit much farther forward on their struts. Designers are taking advantage of the engine thrust which increases air pressure below the wing to improve wing performance.

The flight tests held some pleasant surprises. The drag was lower than expected and the aircraft cruises at Mach 0.84, slightly more than the target of Mach 0.83. That extra speed is enough to chop 15min off the flying time on a flight from Heathrow to Seattle compared to a 767 and 20min off a flight from London to Philadelphia.

True to Boeing tradition, the 777 wing is very big with a long span of 199ft 11in, (60.9m). It is swept back 31.6° and has an area of 4,605sq ft. Because of its long span, the 777 did not need winglets which are typically used to eke out the last bit of performance from an old wing design. The long span also cuts induced drag and gives the 777 improved take-off performance and payload and range. The wing's large area allows the 777 to cruise at altitudes up to 43,000ft and gives it the ability to carry full passenger loads out of many high-elevation, high-temperature airfields.

Although key to the aircraft's performance in the air, some carriers feared the long wing would be a headache on the ground.

The 777's wingspan is more than 30ft wider than the DC-10s it is meant to replace. Airlines wanted the 777's wing to take up no more room than the wingspan of the DC-10s, L-1011s and 767s so that the new aircraft could use existing gates and taxiway space. In response, Boeing initially tried to limit the wingspan to 170ft but this made for an inefficient wing and restricted the aircraft's future growth. So instead, they came up with an elegant solution common on naval aircraft for decades — folding wingtips. A hinge and actuation mechanism will enable about 22ft of each wingtip to fold upward, reducing the wingspan to about 155ft. By late 1996 though, no carrier had ordered the folding wingtip option.

3. Engines

Getting the 777 off the ground required a new breed of jet engines with thrust ratings of 74,500lb to 90,000lb, the largest and most powerful ever used on a commercial aircraft.

For engine manufacturers, it meant having to develop high-thrust powerplants capable of producing 15,000lb to 30,000lb more thrust than those already flying. The engineering required to build these remarkable engines was just as daunting as designing the aircraft itself. Despite the challenges, each of the three major engine manufacturers designed an engine for the 777: the PW4000 development from Pratt & Whitney; General Electric's GE90; and the Trent 800 from Rolls-Royce. The base model 777 is powered by engines rated at 74,000lb to 77,000lb of thrust. As the 777 grew, the engines have been developed to produce even higher thrust — up to 98,000lb — for higher take-off weights and improved payload and ranges. As noted in Boeing's *Airliner* magazine, these new turbofans deliver six times the thrust, a 40% improvement in fuel consumption and have nearly twice the thrust-to-weight ratio compared to engines that launched the jet age. The thrust of a single 777 engine alone easily exceeds all four Pratt &

Whitney JT3C-6 engines — each rated at 13,500lb of thrust — which were on Boeing's first commercial jet, the 707.

Even when compared against newer turbofan engines, the 777 engines produce upwards of 40% more power but are just as quiet as the engines on the 767. That's a big consideration for operations at noise sensitive airports like Heathrow. The benefits of fuel efficiency and noise reduction come from the larger-diameter fans with wide-chord fan blade designs and bypass ratios ranging from 6:1 to as high as 9:1. This compares to 5:1 typical of existing wide-body engines. Like all twin-engined jet aircraft, the 777 is purposely overpowered. This excess thrust provides the necessary margin of safety which enables a 777 to lose an engine at the most critical

Right:
The engines that power the 777 are the most powerful ever fitted to a commercial jetliner. *Boeing*

point on take-off and still have enough power to get airborne on the remaining engine.

The sheer size of the 777 engines is impressive. The giant fan at the front acts like a huge propeller to draw huge amounts of air into the engine, up to two million cubic feet of air per minute at take-off power. That is enough to suck the air out of a four-bedroom house in less than half a second, according to Pratt & Whitney.

Air leaving the fan section is separated into two streams. Some of the air enters the engine core, passing through a series of compressors which boost its pressure up to 30 times the ambient air pressure. This pressurized air then flows into the combustion chamber where it is mixed with vaporized fuel and ignited. The hot exhaust gases expand rapidly and as they exit the engine, they pass through turbines which turn shafts to drive the compressors and the fan. As the turbines spin, they turn the compressors up front, drawing more air into the engine. The larger, second stream of air flows around the engine core, thus the term

high-bypass engine. The GE90 engine on the 777 for example has a bypass ratio of 9:1 — for every part of air that enters the core, nine parts pass through the fan blades and around the core. Accelerated by the front fan and the shape of the engine nacelle, the bypass air provides a significant portion of the total thrust because of its large volume — 90% of the thrust in the PW4084. The cooler bypass air also has the benefit of surrounding the hot exhaust air, muffling the noise and making the engine much quieter than earlier generation jets.

Engine operation is controlled by a full authority digital electronic control (FADEC) system. At the heart of this system is the electronic engine control (EEC) which controls

PW4000 112-INCH FAN ENGINE

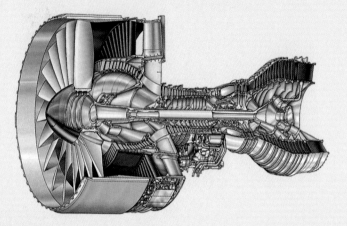

Above:
Cutaway of the Pratt & Whitney 4084. *Pratt & Whitney.*

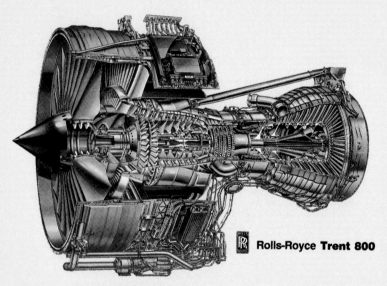

Rolls-Royce Trent 800

Above:
Cutaway of the Rolls-Royce Trent 800. *Rolls-Royce.*

fuel flow, thrust reversers, starting, ignition, fuel and oil cooling, compressor airflow and turbine cooling. The thrust ratings of the engines can be easily changed by making software changes to the EEC.

Testing
Before the engines ever took to the air, they were first subjected to thousands of hours of gruelling operation on test rigs to demonstrate reliability under extreme temperatures and speeds and the ability to withstand potentially catastrophic conditions.

In the dramatic blade-out test, a small explosive bolt is used to sever a fan blade from the disc while the engine is running at full power. The demanding test is done to demonstrate that the fan casing is strong enough to contain the blade fragments and the engine can run out-of-balance until it can be safely shut down. In the case of the GE90, the bolt was detonated at a fan speed of 2,485rpm with the engine producing more than 105,000lb of thrust. The force of the blade's impact on the engine casing was equal to a full-size car hitting a brick wall at 80mph.

Above:
The PW4084 has a 112in diameter, 18in larger than the PW4000 engines on the 747, with 22 wide-chord fan blades. Base models of the engine produce 74,000lb to 77,000lb of thrust with future models producing 98,000lb. *Pratt & Whitney*

The 777 engines also had to pass new, tougher FAA standards which increased the weight of the birds used in bird ingestion tests. In the medium bird test, the engines had to ingest four 2.5lb bird carcasses — fired in a sequential volley to simulate a flock of birds — and continue to produce 75% power and respond to throttle commands for 20min after ingestion. For the large bird test, a single 8lb bird, up from 4lb under previous standards, was fired into the engines at more than 200mph. In this test, there must be no uncontained damage and no fire and the engine must operate for 15sec to permit a controlled shutdown.

In addition to these trials, the engines were run for thousands of hours on ground

rigs at maximum operating temperatures and sometimes intentionally unbalanced to replicate the rigours of day-to-day flying. These cyclic tests ran through the thrust settings of a typical flight — idle, take-off, maximum climb and reverse thrust — all within 5min.

One key element for ETOPS approval was a 3,000-cycles ground test programme, equal to about three to four years of airline service. The engines were put through simulated single-engine diversions when they were run at maximum thrust for up to 180min at a time as if powering an aircraft that had shut down one of its two engines. Finally, each of the engine models flew a 1,000-cycle programme on a 777 to demonstrate reliability in a simulated airline operating environment.

Pratt & Whitney 4084

The Pratt & Whitney 4084 was the launch engine for the 777. It is derived from the PW4000 family of engines — the PW4056 powers the 747-400 and the PW4060 is on the 767 — which has logged more than 14 million hours in service since its introduction in 1987.

Work on the PW4084 began in late 1989 when it became clear that a significant increase in power would be required for the new aircraft. Rather than building a new engine however, Pratt & Whitney chose to build a derivative of its proven PW4000 design since service readiness and reliability were key considerations.

The most obvious difference in the PW4084 is its size. Its fan has a 112in diameter, 18in larger than the PW4000 engines on the 747, with 22 wide-chord fan blades. The two-spool engine has a core common to earlier PW4000 series engines with an 11-stage high pressure (HP) compressor, a combustor and a two-stage high pressure turbine.

Changes to the low pressure (LP) section produced the extra thrust. The six-stage LP compressor has two extra stages over earlier PW4000 engines to increase pressure and the seven-stage LP turbine has three more stages to drive the much larger fan. The engine has a bypass ratio of 6:4.

The first PW4084 was completed on 1 July

1992 and the following month was run at levels in excess of 90,000lb thrust. In all, 22 PW4084 engines were devoted to the test programme. Ground and flight test engines ran more than 14,000hr and the equivalent of 25,000 flight cycles. Seven engines were tested in an altitude test facility. Despite these rigorous ground tests, some at Boeing pushed for in-flight testing to demonstrate the engine's operation through its intended flight envelope.

The challenge was finding an aircraft capable of flying the heavier, larger diameter engines that could also provide a margin of safety in case the test engine failed. Boeing did not have to look far. The choice was a 25-year-old 747, RA001, which had been the first jumbo jet ever to fly. The aircraft was leased from its current owner, Seattle's Museum of Flight, and modified to accommodate the larger engine, including the design of a new strut. The added weight of the test engine caused the wing to droop by 2in and was compensated by adding more fuel to the opposite wing to counterbalance the weight. Some of the older systems in the 747 also had to be updated to interface with the new technology instrument readings from the 4084 engine.

The engine was first flown on the flying test-bed on 9 November 1993. The month-long programme logged 56 flight hours in 17 flights that tested the engine's operation during stalls, sideslips, windmill relights, and inlet angles of attack that exceeded 30°.

The argument whether to do air testing seemed validated in dramatic fashion on the third flight when the engine surged on take-off. The surge, or backfire, was caused by a reversal of air through the engine and produced several loud booms and a flash of flame. Pratt & Whitney officials say the engine had been subjected to a series of gruelling ground tests, including 50 stalls, which degraded its performance. Still, Pratt & Whitney changed clearances in some of the compressor sections and stiffened the engine casing to avoid a repeat of the surge. The PW4084 went on to have a stellar flight-test programme, powering the five 777s used for base certification and the effort to have 180min ETOPS approval for the start of revenue service for the Pratt & Whitney/777 combination.

The engine was certified at 84,000lb thrust in April 1994 and rated at 77,200lb for the first United Airlines 777. By comparison the first engine for the 747, the Pratt & Whitney JT9D, produced 43,000lb.

Pratt & Whitney's PW4084 launched 777 commercial service on 7 June 1995 and in the year that followed 17 Pratt & Whitney-powered 777s were delivered to United, All Nippon Airways and Japan Airlines. In that first year, PW4084 engines logged more than 70,000hr in 21,000 flight cycles with an engine dispatch reliability of nearly 100%.

The heavier model of the 777-200 and the 777-300 stretched version will be powered by the PW4090, a 90,000lb thrust engine. The engine had its first flight in August 1996 and was scheduled to enter service on first deliveries of the 777-200 increased gross weight (IGW) model to United Airlines and Korean Air in early 1997. Other airlines that have chosen the PW4090 include All Nippon Airways for its 10 777-300s; EgyptAir for its three IGW versions and Japan Airlines for its five 777-300s.

Work is also underway on an even higher thrust variant, the PW4098. For this engine, the PW4090 will be modified further with changes to the aerodynamics of the 112in fan to increase airflow and the addition of a single stage to the low pressure compressor to achieve 98,000lb of thrust. The development plan called for certification in 1997 and service in mid-1998 on the 777-300, which has a gross weight of 660,000lb, and later on heavier versions of the IGW model.

Trent 800

Like Pratt & Whitney, Rolls-Royce opted to go with an upgrade of a lower thrust engine as its offering for the 777 rather than develop an entirely new design. The result is the Trent series of engines, the third generation of the RB211 programme that dates back to the early 1970s. The RB211-22B, rated at 42,000lb thrust, first flew on the Lockheed L-1011. Most recently, the engine had evolved into the RB211-524G/H that produce in the range of 60,000lb thrust for use on the 747-400 and 767.

Engineering on the Trent design started in the late 1980s when it became clear that a more powerful engine would be needed for the Airbus A330 and the 777. The Trent 800, capable of thrust ratings of 75,000lb to 95,000lb, was developed for the Boeing 777 while the smaller Trent 700 at 68,000lb to 72,000lb thrust was designed to power the Airbus A330. Both engines are designed for further growth when the market demands.

The main difference of the Trent 800 over its predecessors is the fan size which grows to 110in from 86in. Consequently, the bypass ratio has increased to 6:4, up from about 4:3. To ensure reliability, Rolls purposely kept the operating parameters close to engines already in service; the Trent 800 operates only about 100° Celsius hotter than the -524G/H.

Unlike the other two engines that power the 777, the Trent 800 is a three-spool design. Rolls says each spool runs closer to its optimum speed, enabling compression to be achieved with fewer compressor stages driven by fewer turbine stages. It also allows for a shorter, more rigid engine with good growth potential, as shown by the RB211, which has grown by 53,000lb of thrust since its introduction.

The extra spool for the Trent is an intermediate pressure shaft connecting an eight-stage intermediate pressure (IP) compressor with a single-stage intermediate turbine. One extra stage has been added to the previous RB211 IP compressor to help boost the overall pressure ratio to 40:1. The high pressure spool has a six-stage HP compressor and a single-stage HP turbine. Two extra stages have been added to the LP turbine, which is now five stages, to turn the bigger fan.

Above right:
The first Rolls-Royce-powered 777 flew on 26 May 1995 from Paine Field. *Boeing*

Right:
Thai Airways International was the launch customer for the Rolls-Royce Trent 800 engine, a third generation derivative of the RB211 line. *Rolls-Royce*

The 110in fan has 26 wide-chord blades, a feature pioneered by Rolls-Royce on its RB211-535E4 engine that entered service on the Boeing 757 in 1984. The big blades are more aerodynamically efficient, provide more thrust (cleaner airflow gives more thrust) and are stronger than narrow-chord blades because each blade is larger and more capable of withstanding foreign object damage. When debris enters the engine, the wide-chord blades work like a paddle to deflect the objects harmlessly into the bypass duct and away from the core.

The blades are made from hollow titanium and combine the advantages of strength and light weight, a significant factor in making the Trent 800 the lightest engine for the 777. The weight savings are between 5,000lb and 7,500lb per aircraft which translates into payload and range benefits for an airline.

The Trent 800 began engine testing in September 1993, and in January 1994 was run at 106,087lb thrust. The engine was certified a year later in January 1995. Following the unexpected results of the PW4084 on the flying test bed, it was decided the Trent should fly a similar programme. The engine was flown just over 20hr on a 747 and performed well in a series of tests that included full power take-offs up to 90,000lb thrust, relights, violent throttle movements and extreme aircraft manoeuvres.

The flight test programme then moved to two Cathay Pacific 777s (WA101/VR-HNA and WA102/VR-HNB) for basic certification and 1,000-flight cycle testing of the Rolls-Royce engine/airframe combination. After the initial flights, cracks were discovered on the rear fairings of the strut that holds the engine to the wing. The cause was traced to a tone coming from within the bypass duct which generated a high energy excitation powerful enough to vibrate the entire rear engine structure and crack the non-load-bearing panels. Boeing made some modifications to clean up the aerodynamics and eliminate the fluttering.

The initial 777 requirements were for an engine around 80,000lb thrust but the requirement increased during development to an 84,000lb thrust engine. However the Trent 800 was so successful that Rolls-Royce was able to certify the engine at 90,000lb from the outset. Flight-testing by Boeing revealed greater take-off and cruise thrust and the engine was renamed the Trent 892 to reflect the additional performance.

The 777 powered by the Trent 800 rated at 90,000lb won type certification from the FAA and Joint Aviation Authorities in February 1996. The first Trent-powered 777 entered service with Thai Airways International that April, followed a month later by Cathay Pacific and then in June, by Emirates.

The 1,000-cycle programme for ETOPS approval was halted for about a month in the summer of 1996 when an engine surge forced an aborted take-off. WA102, the ETOPS aircraft, had completed 886 cycles and was performing hot weather operations at Mesa, Arizona, when the surge occurred at low speed on the runway. An investigation confirmed that the surge was caused by the loss of a HP compressor blade which had suffered foreign object damage from a previous bird strike. Smear marks on five fan blade roots confirmed that the engine had ingested a medium or large bird into the core, larger indeed than what was required during the bird strike tests done for certification.

Cathay crews joined the ETOPS programme for 90 flights, totalling about 400hr, to destinations in the airline's route structure such as Hong Kong, Bangkok, Sydney and Christchurch, New Zealand. The ETOPS programme was completed at the end of July 1996, after logging 1,318hr. Formal approval for 180min ETOPS was granted in October 1996.

Rolls-Royce is offering the Trent 892 for both the longer range, increased gross weight model and the stretched model 777. The first Rolls-powered IGW model was scheduled to begin revenue service with Emirates in 1997. The 777-300 stretched version is to enter service with Cathay in May 1998. Rolls has committed itself to the higher thrust Trent 895, tentatively slated for revenue service in mid-1999, to extend the operational flexibility of the 777-300. This thrust level is also well suited to further weight increases under consideration for the 777-200. A Trent capable of 100,000lb thrust is also under development.

By late 1996, Rolls-Royce had captured about 35% of the engine business for the 777. In addition to Thai and Cathay, the engine has been selected by Emirates, Malaysia Airlines and Singapore Airlines, which alone has placed orders for 28 777s and options for an additional 33, a deal worth $1.8 billion to the British engine maker.

Above:
The GE90 logged just over 200hr on GE's flying test-bed, a 747-100 once flown by Pan Am. *GE*

GE90

The only all-new engine design to power the 777 is the GE90 from GE Aircraft Engines. It was a huge gamble and as GE would find out, not without its share of trials. But GE believed that an all-new engine would have the best growth potential and give it a technological edge in the race to power other big jets of the future.

As the company's first new base-line engine for large commercial aircraft in more than 20 years, the GE90 incorporates new technology featuring wide-chord composite blades and a new combustor design and high pressure compressor.

The engine was designed, developed and produced by GE Aircraft Engines with participation from Snecma, of France, its partner on the successful CFM 56 engine, Ishikawajima-Harima Heavy Industries, of Japan, and Fiat Avio of Italy.

The fortunes of the GE90 got a huge boost when British Airways, for years a loyal Rolls-Royce customer, announced in 1991 that it had selected the GE90. With an initial order for 15 777s and options for another 15, the British carrier became the launch customer for the GE engine. Other airlines that have selected the GE90 include China Southern, Continental Airlines, Euralair, Lauda Air, Saudia and International Lease Finance Corporation.

The GE90 is the world's largest engine: at 123in, the diameter of its fan is about equal to the fuselage of the Boeing 727. The large fan produces a high bypass ratio of 9:1, a key factor in making the engine the quietest of those on the 777. The GE90 has an overall pressure ratio of 40:1. Like the PW4084, the GE90 is a two-spool engine. The LP shaft has the 123in fan, a three-stage LP compressor and a six-stage LP turbine. The HP shaft has a 10-stage HP compressor connected to a two-stage HP turbine.

The GE90 marks the first use of big fan blades made from composite materials. But GE knew the advantages of composite blades because of earlier work it had done using the technology, like the GE36 Unducted Fan, or

Above:
Unlike the other engines that power the 777, the Trent 800 is a three-spool design, which allows each spool to run closer to its optimum speed, according to the British engine maker. *Rolls-Royce*

Above right:
Cutaway of the GE90. *GE*

Right:
The Trent 800 flew five flights for a total of just over 20hr on a 747 test-bed. *Rolls-Royce*

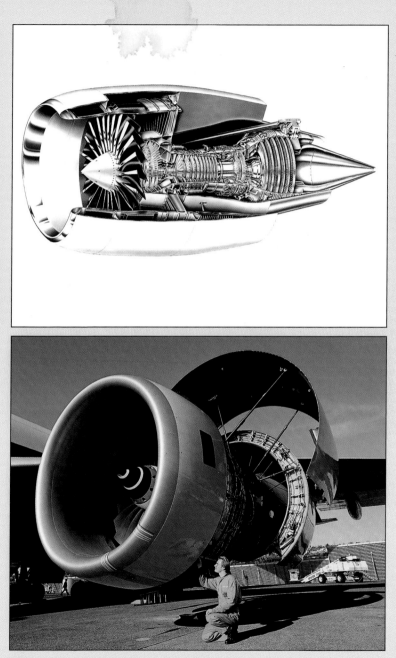

UDF. The UDF, with its rear composite fan blades, logged more than 700hr of testing on a Boeing 727 and MD-80 in the 1980s. One benefit is the light weight of the blades, a crucial factor when the fan is so much bigger than previous powerplants. And in the event the fan loses a blade, the composite blades make containment easier and the imbalance less pronounced than a heavier titanium blade. As well, the composite blades, fitted with a titanium leading edge guard, offer good protection against bird strikes and are less susceptible to dangerous fatigue cracking that can propagate from small nicks and tears typically caused by foreign object damage, according to GE.

GE put the new blades through an extensive test programme to ensure the composite materials would withstand typical wear and tear. On an outdoor test stand, the blades were rigged to a CFM56-3 engine and then subjected to monsoon rain ingestion at take-off power, equal to 225gal of water per minute, and 15min of hailstone ingestion totalling 900lb of hail. The blades were free of damage and erosion after the tests.

The GE90 features a new dual-dome combustor design which has two burner zones arranged in a ring around the engine. At low power settings before take-off only the outer, or pilot burner operates, to create fewer emissions, especially hydrocarbons and carbon monoxide. At higher power settings, both the pilot and main burners operate to cut emissions of nitrous oxide and smoke.

The engine's specific fuel consumption is 8-10% lower than current high bypass turbofans. GE says that replacing a 747 with

Right:
The GE90 marks the first time that the fan blades have been made from composite materials instead of titanium. *Author*

Above right:
The first GE-powered Boeing 777 had a successful first flight on 2 February 1995. Despite their huge thrust, the new engines generate only about a third of the noise footprint of the newest 747s on take-off. *Boeing*

a GE90-powered twin on long-range routes would save one million gallons of fuel a year.

GE announced development of the new engine in January 1990 and by November 1992, testing had begun on the engine core. Testing on the first full GE90 engine began in March 1993 and later that year initial flight testing started on a modified 747-100 formerly operated by Pan Am. The engine would eventually fly 228hr on the testbed. The first GE90-powered 777 had its maiden flight on 2 February 1995 and the engines performed flawlessly during the 5hr 20min flight. Certification of the GE90 used two 777s destined for British Airways (WA076/ G-ZZZA and WA077/G-ZZZB). WA076 was the first GE90-powered 777 to fly and was used for standard certification testing. WA077 flew the 1,000-cycle validation needed for ETOPS approval for the GE90/777 combination.

Testing ran into some turbulence in May 1995. In one incident, a GE90 surged during flight testing. Then just a few weeks later, a bird-strike test on the 92,000lb thrust version of the engine in a ground rig revealed a greater than expected imbalance. The blades survived the bird strike okay but the aluminium retainers at the base of the blade were too rigid and cut into the blade in the impact. The two incidents forced a halt in the flight test programme and sent GE engineers

scrambling to first figure out what caused the problems and then to fix them.

The solution to the engine surge was a modification to the engine's electronic control system that automatically controls the stators, or small vanes in the engine that guide airflow. To solve the problem uncovered by the bird strike, GE modified the aluminium spacers which ensure a smooth aerodynamic flow between the blades. The strike test was successfully completed just over a month later, paving the way for the resumption of certification flight testing in July after a hiatus of more than a month.

But these problems and other questions surrounding icing, composite blades and blade-out tests delayed certification and the scheduled September delivery of the first GE-powered 777 to British Airways. The 777 powered by the GE90-85B was certified on 9 November 1995, marking the completion of a test programme that involved 13 engines and more than 19,000 cycles in ground and flight testing. The 84,700lb thrust engine derated to 76,400lb entered revenue service with British Airways that same month on flights to the Gulf region. In its first six months of service, six 777s flown by British Airways and China Southern had logged 16,000hr on GE90 engines with no inflight shutdowns and a 99.97% dispatch rate.

Above:
Engineers at Boeing Field open up the nacelle of the more powerful GE90-92B engine after a test flight. This engine, rated at 92,000lb thrust, powers the increased gross weight model of the 777-200. *Author*

The next hurdle was successfully crossed in August 1996, when the GE/777 combination completed the 1,000-cycle flight test programme needed for 180min ETOPS approval. Regulatory approval was granted that October.

The growth potential for GE90 was clearly shown when the GE90-85 was operated regularly at more than 100,000lb during testing. At one point, the engine produced 110,300lb on the test stand and GE officials claimed a record for the highest thrust ever reached by a high bypass turbofan engine. The higher thrust GE90-92B was certified by the FAA in July 1996 at 92,000lb of thrust, the most powerful engine ever certified by the agency.

The -92B required only minimal changes to produce the extra power: the high pressure turbine has extra cooling features and a thermal barrier coating on stage 1 blades. New materials are used in the low pressure turbine. As it was for the base GE90 engine, British Airways was also the launch airline for the first IGW model powered by the GE90-92B derated to 85,000lb. The engine and aircraft began flight testing in October and delivery to the British airline was expected in early 1997. Also under development is the GE90-100B, a 100,000lb thrust engine which will be derated to 98,000lb in service.

An All Nippon Airways Boeing 777. *Boeing*

65

4. Roll-out to Revenue Service

There was no traditional roll-out ceremony for the first 777; rather the jet was unveiled in a grand style suited to the scale of the aircraft itself. On 9 April 1994, Boeing showed off its new pride and joy to 100,000 people in 15 separate ceremonies over the day at its Everett plant, the largest such event ever staged by the manufacturer.

The first aircraft was christened 'Working Together' and in that theme most of those invited were the very people who had made the day possible — the employees who had worked on the project and their families.

The guests, 7,000 at a time, were treated to an elaborately staged light show and video presentation in a darkened portion of the assembly hall. Then a curtain was raised and they were ushered forward for a closer look at the aircraft, painted in the familiar red, white and blue Boeing livery. Splashed in lights on a wall behind the aircraft were the names of the 777 customers. By this point, Boeing had 147 firm orders from 16 airlines for the 777; 98 were for the

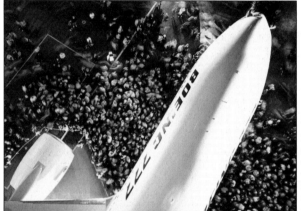

Left and below:
The first Boeing 777 was unveiled to 100,000 guests — and the world — during a day-long series of ceremonies on 9 April 1994. *Boeing*

Left:
The flight test programme started with taxying trials to confirm steering and braking.
Boeing

Below:
Flight testing involved nine 777s in all, six for type certification and another three which flew 1,000-cycle programmes to earn 180min ETOPS approval for each of the engine/airframe combinations.
Boeing

A-version and 49 were for the B-version.

That evening the first 777, known as WA001, was towed out of the factory and onto the Boeing flight line at adjacent Paine Field in preparation for the next big milestone: first flight.

The flight tests started modestly with low-speed taxying to check steering and braking and engine operation. Then moving to the runway at Paine Field, the taxi trials progressed to higher speeds so the pilots could test the flight controls — using rudder to yaw the nose, elevator to lift the nosewheel off the runway and ailerons to lift a wing.

Finally, they had tested everything that could be tested on the ground and the day had come for first flight on 12 June 1994.

With pilots John Cashman and Ken Higgins at the controls, the big jet lined up on the runway at Paine Field. The aircraft weighed 428,289lb, including 119,460lb of fuel. The take-off was normal and within minutes, the 777 disappeared from view into the grey clouds that hung low over the airport.

After take-off, the flight crew turned the aircraft east, over the Cascade Mountains, in search of better weather. The first task was to explore basic handling using normal and back-up modes of the fly-by-wire system. Then they checked the operation of the landing gear and flaps. And in tests not usually performed on a first flight, the big jet was slowed to buffet speed, at the edge of a stall, at all flap speeds, and one engine was shut-down and relit. The aircraft reached 20,000ft and the speed was limited to 250kt.

No one really expected any surprises since the aircraft and its engines had been so extensively tested on the ground. Still, no one takes a maiden flight for granted and there were plenty of smiling faces when the 777 appeared out of the clouds and floated in for a smooth touch-down.

The flight lasted 3hr 48min, a record for an all-new Boeing jet. Both pilots were delighted with the jet's performance and reported a smooth maiden flight. In fact, once in the clouds, the two pilots joked it was just like the simulator. Just two small problems were encountered: buffeting in the nosewheel doors and trailing-edge flap buffeting at low speed during the landing approach, both of which were corrected later on.

Flight Testing

The first flight marked the beginning of the 777's flight test programme — the most rigorous ever undertaken by Boeing — to

prove the jet was reliable, service-ready and certified for ETOPS flights. The flight test effort involved nine 777s in all — six devoted to the type certification of the airframe and the Pratt & Whitney, Rolls-Royce and General Electric engines. Another three aircraft flew the 1,000-cycles programmes needed to certify each of the three engine/airframe combinations for ETOPS flights.

Launch customer United Airlines had selected Pratt & Whitney engines, so the base certification for the 777-200 was done using four aircraft powered by PW4084 engines, including aircraft No 1 owned by Boeing and three others that would eventually go to United. The second 777 flew on 15 July 1994 and by December 1994, five aircraft were flying test flights.

The first 777 was devoted to basic aerodynamic testing; flight controls, stalls, runway performance and brake work. The second and third 777s were used to test autopilots, aircraft systems and air conditioning. The fourth aircraft was devoted to the 1,000-cycle programme for ETOPS approval. The No 5 jet was used to test the complex set-up of the in-flight passenger entertainment system. To do this, the jet had a full passenger layout except in the aft section where a small collection of data equipment was located.

The test aircraft would have to fly 80hr a month per aircraft to complete the 10-month test programme on time. The best Boeing had ever done before was just over 40hr.

Major test activities for base certification included:
• Aerodynamics: measuring the aircraft's performance during take-off and landing and its drag characteristics. The aircraft was flown to the edges of its envelope, from overspeed to stalls.
• Stability and control: testing the aircraft's flying qualities at various speeds, altitudes, weights and flap settings.
• Autoflight controls: confirming the operation of the autopilot, flight director, autothrottle and flight management systems.
• Structures: evaluating the structural response to 'flutter' testing and verifying loads on the airframe.
• Systems: checking avionics, electrical, air conditioning, brakes and aspects of engine operation, such as start-up and fuel consumption.

Above:
The tail of a 777 kicks up a trail of dust and smoke as it is purposely dragged along the runway during the dramatic velocity minimum unsticks tests. These trials are done to determine minimum take-off speeds and develop the take-off performance used by airlines. *Boeing*

Below:
Demanding brake tests were done at Edwards Air Force Base to demonstrate that the brakes could stop a fully laden 777 after a rejected take-off. *Boeing*

Above:
By late 1994, the flight test programme was well underway with five test aircraft logging nearly 80hr a month each, far more than any previous test programme. *Boeing*

Below:
The first 777 with Rolls-Royce engines is prepared for its maiden flight in the spring of 1995. *Cathay Pacific*

To record and monitor the flight test activities, the first three 777s, as well as the first GE and Rolls-Royce 777s, were outfitted with 22 racks of computer consoles and instrumentation that tracked more than 50,000 parameters, everything from hydraulic pressures and airspeed to electrical signals, temperatures and pressures. These data systems weighed about 34,000lb and required more than 100 miles of wiring. Also on board were four dozen 55gal water barrels, half in the front cabin, the rest in the rear. The barrels were used to simulate the weight of passengers and cargo and to alter aircraft's centre of gravity by pumping water forward or aft.

Following the initial flights, the test programme shifted to Boeing Field, located just south of Seattle, which is home to Boeing's delivery centre. By early July, WA001 had logged more than 100hr of testing. Those first few weeks were spent assessing the

aircraft's controls and handling qualities and exploring the flight envelope. The aircraft also completed flutter tests to check the structure response to high speeds.

In the autumn of 1994, WA001 was flown to Edwards Air Force Base, California, the legendary home of test flying, for a series of flights to evaluate take-off performance and brake testing. With a 15,000ft runway set on a dry lake bed in the Mojave Desert, Edwards provided a good safety buffer for these more risky flights. The aircraft completed the first major FAA certification tests when it performed tests for VMU (velocity minimum unsticks). In this test, the aircraft was rotated to the maximum angle of attack at about 95kt, well below the safe rotation speed of 130 to 165kt depending on weight. The aircraft's tail, protected by an oak skid, was deliberately dragged on the runway before the jet lifted off at the lowest possible airspeed. The test is done to determine minimum take-off speeds and develop the take-off performance used by airlines. Rotating a jet prematurely on take-off can put the aircraft into such an extreme nose high attitude that the combination of excessive drag and weight prevents it from lifting off.

Also at Edwards, the jet did increasingly heavy take-offs and rejected take-offs on wet and dry runway surfaces, all leading up to the most demanding test of all — a rejected take-off at maximum weight and maximum speed to demonstrate that the brakes could stop a fully-loaded 777.

This test is for the rare emergency when a pilot has to stop an aircraft at the worst possible time during its take-off roll, just before the aircraft has reached the V1 decision speed. If the jet suffers a serious emergency before this speed the take-off is rejected and maximum braking applied. Past this speed, the aircraft is committed to flight. A rejected take-off can be a tricky manoeuvre itself and is reserved for the most serious emergencies that threaten an aircraft's ability to fly.

Boeing tested for the worst case to ensure a margin of safety for the airlines. The brakes were purposely worn down to the point of replacement and the aircraft was laden with fuel to 632,500lb, the maximum weight of the higher gross weight B-model and heavier than the base model would ever be in service. The aircraft was lined up on the runway and engines throttled up to 88,000lb of thrust. As the aircraft reached 183kt, the pilots applied maximum braking and retarded the throttles.

Without the use of thrust reversers, the aircraft stopped in about 12,800ft of runway, about 1,400ft less than expected. The brakes glowed a fiery orange-red from the all-out effort, their temperatures going off the scale at 3,000° Celsius. One by one, the 12 main tyres deflated as heat-sensitive fuse plugs melted to allow the controlled release of tyre pressure and prevent an explosive blow-out. Though standing by, the firefighters could not intervene for 5min. This simulated the typical reaction time of airport fire crews and demonstrated that no major fires would break out.

The brake trials were a success and the jet went on to fly a test programme that

explored the full flight envelope. Boeing pilots did full stalls at all flap settings, throughout the centre of gravity, in turns and with power on and off. It could take 5,000ft to recover from stalls with flaps up and at heavier weights.

In March 1995, WA001 was used for a series of tests to determine the configuration deviation lists. These list components that, if removed, will not disrupt aerodynamic performance or handling. During the tests, the 777 was flown with a variety of parts missing, including fairings, exterior light lenses, access panels, wingtip fairings and the seals on the leading edge flaps.

Boeing was reminded at several points that test flying is not routine. Early in the programme, a small access panel came off and severed a hydraulic hose during a test to retract the landing gear at high speed. Fluid quickly drained from the hydraulic system, one of three on the aircraft, that powers the gear and some of the wing surfaces. The gear could not be retracted or locked into place using normal procedures. Pilot John Cashman rolled the aircraft slightly to ensure the side braces on the main wheels were locked into place before making an uneventful landing.

Then in February 1995, the FAA imposed an altitude restriction of 25,000ft after two incidents of rapid decompression within a day

Left:

A United Airlines 777 pays a visit to Vancouver International Airport during certification. *Jim Jorgenson*

Below:

A Pratt & Whitney-powered jet logged 1,284hr during the unprecedented 1,000-cycle ETOPS programme with flight times varying from under an hour to more than nine hours. *Boeing*

of each other. The problem was traced to the failure of a clamp and safety check valve in the pressurization system. In one incident, seven members of the test team were injured when WA002 lost cabin pressure at 42,000ft over the Seattle area.

WA004, also a United Airlines 777, had its first flight on 28 October 1994, and that December began flying a special 1,000-cycle validation programme to get early ETOPS approval. It was an unprecedented exercise involving a team of several hundred engineers, pilots and technicians drawn from Boeing, the airlines, engine manufacturers and the FAA.

This programme — the equivalent of more than a year of flights for a typical airline — was designed as a simulation of airline-type flight operations and maintenance procedures to demonstrate the reliability needed for daily service, including ETOPS flights. Each cycle included the components of a typical airline flight: engine start, taxi, take-off, climb, cruise, descent, approach and landing. Eventually, three 777s flew a 1,000-cycle programme, one for each of the engine models, and all were equipped with a full passenger configuration as if in revenue service.

The Pratt & Whitney-powered jet logged 1,284hr during its 1,000-cycle testing with flight times varying from under an hour to more than 9hr. The first 500 cycles were flown using an 'aged' PW4084 engine that had already flown 2,000 simulated flights in ground testing. The aircraft also performed eight 180min single-engine diversions for a total of 24hr.

The experience gained through this extensive programme was far more varied than what a typical 777 would be exposed to in a single year of airline service. The 777s were baked and frozen during flights to New Mexico, Arizona, Montana, Alaska and Sweden to test the operation of aircraft systems in temperatures ranging from -44°F to 108°F.

In April 1995, United Airlines flight and ground crew took part in the last 90 cycles of the 1,000-cycle programme to prepare for the jet's introduction to the United fleet and help the airline obtain the separate regulatory approval it needed for ETOPS flights. Airlines that want to fly the 777 on such long routes must demonstrate that their flight operations, maintenance, flight planning and training can handle the unique requirements of such flights. During this portion of testing, the aircraft logged about 400hr on typical United routes such as Washington DC to Los Angeles; Denver to Miami and Washington DC to Honolulu.

By May 1995, flight testing was well underway on the GE-powered 777. It made its maiden flight in the colours of British Airways on 2 February 1995, flying for 5hr and 20min before landing at Boeing Field. The Trent 800 was also in the air, flying for the first time on a 777 on 26 May 1995 to start a flight test programme that would use two jets in Cathay Pacific Airways livery.

The 777 was being tested on the ground as well. In one critical FAA test of evacuation procedures, Boeing had to demonstrate that passengers could exit a 777 within 90sec using only four of the aircraft's eight doors. The test was done in a darkened hangar at Everett. Inside the cabin, normal lighting was turned off and the emergency lighting came on, signalling the start of the mock evacuation. Passengers had to make their way past luggage and briefcases strewn in the aisles to simulate a real emergency and then down the inflatable slides. After this first test, the 777 was certified to carry 419 passengers, later raised to 440 passengers following a second test.

In another test, volunteer travellers were served a meal in a United Airlines 777 to assess that the carts, trays and galley equipment all worked properly. Although not required for certification, it was an important exercise to ensure happy customers.

Just one month before the first delivery of a 777 to United Airlines, Boeing took WA003 on a three-week tour that covered 45,890 miles through 10 countries. Billed as the World Celebration Tour, it gave government officials, media and more importantly airlines like Asiana, Air China, Air India, South African Airways and Malaysia Airlines a sneak preview of the aircraft.

The first half of the tour started in Seoul, Korea, then on to China with stops in Beijing and Guangzhou, home of China Southern

Airlines, a 777 customer, and Hong Kong and Taipei, Taiwan. On 17 April, the aircraft flew from Seattle to London to begin the second leg of the tour that stopped in Cape Town and Johannesburg, South Africa; Bombay and Delhi in India; Kuala Lumpur, Malaysia; Singapore and finally Bangkok, Thailand. On its 7,850-mile, nonstop flight from Bangkok to Seattle, the jetliner set a new speed record for the route. The 13hr 36min flight was the aircraft's longest flight in distance and time.

Boeing estimated the flight test effort would log almost 7,000hr in more than 4,900 cycles from June 1994 to June 1996. Throughout, the aircraft performed almost flawlessly during the programme, unprecedented in commercial aviation history.

Static and Fatigue Testing

With flight testing underway, two 777s came off the assembly line that would never carry a passenger nor even roll down a runway. These two airframes, minus the engines, were destined for a modern-day version of the medieval rack — static and fatigue testing to evaluate the aircraft's ability to withstand stresses and loadings far greater than it would experience in airline operations.

Eventually, one of the frames was literally pulled apart.

The static tests demonstrate that the aircraft structure can carry the design limit load without causing permanent deformation of the structure. These were done in the final assembly hall at the Everett factory where a 777 airframe was surrounded by a steel framework. Hydraulic actuators applied loads to various parts of the test aircraft as more than 4,300 strain gauges connected by more than 500 miles of wiring measured the forces. These included simulations of positive and negative flight manoeuvres, pressurization, engine thrust loads, ground loads such as landing and taxi, and air loads on slats, flaps, ailerons and spoilers. The flight aircraft were initially limited to 80% of design limit loads

Below:
The static test aircraft was the second airframe off the assembly line. In a test of the aircraft's growth potential, each wing was pulled 24ft above its normal position before breaking. *Boeing*

until static testing proved the structure could withstand the full loads.

The final test came in January 1995, with the wing destruct test which explored the growth potential of the wing design by loading it to the breaking point. This dramatic test, in which the wings are gradually pulled upwards, demonstrated that the 777's design loads provide ample safety margin to handle the most extreme loading that could be experienced. With this confirmed, testing

Above:
Groundcrews prepare the first Boeing 777 for another test flight at Roswell, New Mexico. *Boeing*

Below:
VR-HNA logged 641 hours for the type certification of the Rolls-Royce/airframe combination. *Rolls-Royce*

While the first 777 was being tested in the air, another 777 airframe was 'flown' in a ground test rig for fatigue testing. From January 1995 until March 1997, the aircraft flew about 250 flights a day. Each flight reproduced the loads expected during a 90min flight until the aircraft had experienced two times its minimum design service objective. In the case of the 777, this was the equivalent of 120,000 flights, equal to about 60 years in service. *Boeing*

day, with loads varying in severity and frequency. As well, the cabin was pressurized to 8.6psi with each cycle. The repeated cycles aged the airframe to more than twice its intended service life and enabled Boeing to pinpoint areas that might experience fatigue problems as well as verify inspection and maintenance procedures. The 777 has a design life in excess of 40,000 flights. As of October 1996 fatigue testing had completed 80,000 cycles with no sign of significant problems.

continued until the wings were loaded to 154% of the strongest forces they would ever encounter in flight — equal to about 500,000lb of force on each wing. The wings were pulled 24ft above their normal position when suddenly the wing structure started to buckle and the wings snapped almost simultaneously with a startling bang.

Static tests proved the strength of the airframe. But it was up to fatigue tests to demonstrate the aircraft's ability to withstand loadings more typical of day-to-day operations.

Conducted outside at Boeing's Everett plant, 100 hydraulic actuators pulled and pushed the frame of a 777, simulating the loads of a typical flight, including taxi, take-off, cruise, descent, turbulence and landing. A flight cycle was applied every 4min, 24hr a

Into Service

The 777 received type certification from the FAA and European Joint Aviation Authorities (JAA) on 19 April 1995, confirming the Pratt & Whitney-powered version of the jet met the latest safety requirements and was ready to enter service in the USA and Europe. The first 777 was delivered to United Airlines on 15 May 1995. Two weeks later, on 30 May, the Pratt & Whitney-powered 777 got FAA approval for 180min ETOPS, permitting US carriers to fly the aircraft on routings 3hr flying time from an alternate airport. That means the 777 can fly virtually unrestricted around the world, except for a small corner of the Pacific Ocean. The JAA granted the aircraft 120min ETOPS approval. It was the first time an aircraft had been okayed to fly long, over-water routes from its first day in service. But the push for early ETOPS approval

had not been without controversy though. Critics questioned whether Boeing was pushing the safety envelope and some even charged that the FAA was too cosy with the big aircraft maker.

The question for the FAA was whether technology and testing could be trusted to work all the bugs out of an aircraft design, a process that previously had been left to in-service experience. But there was no disputing that the 777 had been exhaustively tested. By the time of delivery to United Airlines, five Pratt & Whitney-powered 777s had completed 1,751 flights totalling 3,379hr, far more than the base certification of the 767, which totalled 1,584 flights and 1,793hr.

Above:
The first 777 off the line for British Airways.
British Airways

Below:
The 777 is a popular sight in Japan. Airlines there have ordered more of the wide-body than any other country and were the impetus for the stretched model. All Nippon has ordered 28 777s. *Boeing*

All the design work, engineering and testing came to fruition on 7 June 1995 when United Airlines Flight 921 departed London's Heathrow Airport for Dulles International

Above:
Japan Airlines has designated its 777s as 'Star Jets' and each is named after a star or constellation. The first aircraft is *Sirius*, named after the brightest star visible from earth at night. It was the 23rd 777 off the production line. *Boeing*

Airport in Washington, DC. It was the first revenue flight of the 777-200. Two other United 777s made inaugural flights the same day — Flight 910 from Denver to Chicago and Flight 940 from Chicago to Frankfurt — marking the culmination of a remarkable process that had started five years earlier. It was perhaps symbolic that two of the three flights that day were ETOPS flights.

With its official launch into service, the 777 started to do what it was designed for — making money for the airlines flying it. United introduced its 777s on an aggressive schedule that included domestic destinations like Chicago, Denver and Washington and across the Atlantic to Frankfurt and London. Triple seven service was later added to the Miami-São Paulo route.

United's 777s are configured to carry 292 passengers in three classes: 12 in first class, 49 in business and 231 in economy. The economy seats are 18½in wide, 1½in wider than the economy seats on the 747-400. United's A-market aircraft have the Pratt & Whitney PW4077 engines — the PW4084

engine derated to the lower thrust.

The airline initially ordered 16 of the A-market jets and 18 increased gross weight (IGW) models and later added two extra orders for the heavier weight aircraft. The IGW models have the range to fly from the USA west coast to Europe, like Los Angeles to London. The airline is now using the longer-range version of the 767s on those routes and the 777 will enable United to capitalize on growing passenger loads.

After just over a year in service, United's 777s were turning in a 98.1% reliability rate, close to the three-year target the airline had set of 98.5%. Each 777 is flying just over 10hr a day. United's fleet of new twinjets had carried 2.2 million passengers for an average load factor of 78%, an indication that the aircraft is well-suited to the routes it was flying. By the end of 1996, the airline had 16 777s in operation and another 14 were to be delivered in 1997. As the 777s entered service, the airline retired three 747-100s and five DC-10-10s in 1996 with a further five 747-100s and five DC-10-10s to be disposed of in 1997.

Across the Pacific Ocean, Japan has the world's most heavily travelled routes and airlines there have placed more orders for 777s than any other country: 15 for Japan Airlines; 28 for All Nippon Airways (ANA) and seven for Japan Air System.

All Nippon Airways became the second airline to fly the jet when it took delivery of a 777 in October 1995. With 28 777s on order — 18 777-200s and 10 777-300s — ANA will be the second largest operator of 777s and the largest outside the United States. After several months to train flight crews, the 777 started revenue service with ANA on 23 December, flying between Tokyo's Haneda airport and Itami airport in Osaka. In their first six months of operation, All Nippon's 777s had achieved near 100% reliability, virtually unheard of for a new aircraft type, ANA staff report.

ANA's 777s seat 376 passengers, 18 in a 2-2-2 configuration in a domestic business class and 358 in economy in a 3-3-3 arrangement. The aircraft are used exclusively on ANA's busy, short-haul domestic routes; in addition to the Osaka flight, the 777s fly between Tokyo and Sapporo on the north island of Hokkaido. This is the busiest city pairing in the world and the 777s supplement ANA's 747-400s, configured to seat 569 passengers, which also fly the route.

As the new Boeings arrived in the fleet, ANA, once a big operator of Lockheed L-1011s, retired the last of the trijets and expects to do the same with its 747-100s. The airline planned to put its additional 777s into service on intra-Asia routes to China, Korea, Hong Kong and Singapore.

British Airways was originally scheduled to take delivery of its first 777 in late September but had to sit out a delay of several months while extra certification testing was done on the GE90/777 combination. Much to their relief, the GE-powered 777 won FAA certification on 9 November 1995, paving the way for delivery of the 777 to the airline two days later.

Below:
The first 777 in Emirates livery just before its roll-out in Seattle. Emirates' 777s are powered by the Rolls-Royce Trent 870 engine and are configured to seat 303 people — 18 in first, 49 in business and 236 in economy. Each seat has a personal video screen and telephone. *Emirates*

Above right:
Thai Airways International took delivery of its first 777-200 in April 1996. The airline's first aircraft was named *Lamphun* after a Thai province. The aircraft began revenue service two months later on routes from Bangkok to Hong Kong and Seoul. The Bangkok-based carrier has ordered eight 777-200s and six 777-300s. *Boeing*

British Airways wasted no time introducing its new acquisition on routes from London to destinations throughout the Middle East including Dubai, Muscat, Jeddah and Cairo. Its 777s are configured to seat 235 passengers with almost two-thirds of the seating in each aircraft dedicated to first and business class seating, an indication of just how lucrative the Middle East market is.

The GE-powered 777 was granted regulatory approval for 180min ETOPS flights in October 1996, enabling British Airways to begin transatlantic flights with the aircraft between London and Boston that same month. The British carrier has ordered 18 777s and holds options for 15 more. The first five on order are for the base model and 13 remaining aircraft are for the IGW model. The first of the IGW models were delivered in February 1997, for use on the transatlantic market with seating for 267 passengers.

The airline was delighted with the aircraft, reporting an almost flawless introduction with just four delays attributable to engine problems after a year's service. Like other carriers, British Airways was utilizing the 777 on markets that had outgrown the 767.

Delivery of a 777 to China Southern Airlines on 29 December 1995, the first of six 777s it has ordered, rounded off the year.

Japan Airlines received its first 777 in February 1996 and its second in late March and put the new jets into service near the end of April. A third 777 joined the fleet of Japan Airlines, the country's largest carrier, that summer. The 777s are used on domestic service between Haneda airport in Tokyo and three cities on the southern island of Kyushu — Kagoshima, Nagasaki and Fukuoka, this last route being the second busiest city pairing in the world.

The JAL 777s, which seat 12 in domestic first class and another 377 in economy, are used to supplement an already frequent 747 service and replace older 747s at a third less the cost. In addition to the 10 777-200 models on order, the airline has also ordered five stretched 777-300s, with PW4090 engines, to also fly busy Japanese routes together with its 747-400 domestic jumbos.

The Rolls-Royce-powered 777 was certified by the FAA and Europe's JAA in February 1996, paving the way for delivery of the first 777 with Trent 800 engines to Thai Airways International that April. The aircraft, the first of 14 ordered by the airline, was launched on routes from Bangkok to Hong Kong and Seoul.

The first 777 delivery to Cathay Pacific followed the next month and it began flying from the airline's hub in Hong Kong to Bangkok, Tokyo's Narita airport, Seoul and Taipei. Dubai and Bahrain in the Middle East were added to the 777's schedule near the end of 1996. Cathay's 777s seat 343 passengers, just 44 fewer than a 747-400; 50 in a 2-3-2 business configuration and 293 in economy in a 2-5-2 arrangement.

Cathay's 320-seat Airbus A330s were used to replace the Lockheed TriStars which were retired in October 1996, while the 777, with more range and capacity, was used to complement the 747-200s at a substantial saving in fuel and maintenance. Cathay has orders for 11 of the jets — four for the base model and seven for the 777-300 powered by the Trent 892 — as well as options for another 11 of the stretched model.

Cathay reported a smooth entry into service and at one point went six weeks with no technical delays on the three 777s it had at the time. The only wrinkle in the airline's early experience with the new aircraft came just a few months after the first delivery. A 777 was en route to Hong Kong from Bangkok when the pilots got a fire warning for the front cargo hold. The crew discharged

the extinguisher bottles but the warning continued, prompting an emergency evacuation of the aircraft upon landing in Hong Kong. An investigation revealed that the source of the warning was a shipment of frogs in the hold! The fire detection system had trouble distinguishing between smoke and atmospheric moisture. During the flight, the frogs had sweated, raising the humidity level in the confined space and causing the false alarm. Rather than degrade the sensitivity of the detector, one solution was the installation of a heater to warm the air and remove moisture before it got to the detector.

Cathay's 777-300s, with seating for 364, will serve eastern Australia when deliveries start in 1998. Typically, the long-haul flights arrive in Hong Kong in the morning and depart late evening. To maximize use of the 777-300, a typical daily schedule will probably have it operate as a regional flight

Top:
The brushed wing graces Cathay Pacific's third 777 as it is readied on the factory flight line before delivery. Cathay's 777s are equipped with Trent 877 engines. *Boeing*

Above:
Seen here on the ramp at Boeing Field in the autumn of 1996, British Airways aircraft G-ZZZB has been fitted with higher thrust GE90-92B engines for testing. The aircraft, which also flew the 1,000-cycle ETOPS programme for the GE90 engine, was then refurbished and joined revenue service in March 1997. *Author*

to the likes of Tokyo and back during the day and then a long-haul to Melbourne or Sydney that same evening.

First Year

The 777 marked its first year with 23 of the aircraft delivered, 21 in daily service and more than 38,000 flight hours logged on flights to 31 cities around the globe.

Despite unprecedented testing by Boeing, the true test of an aircraft always comes when it enters revenue service. Boeing is not an airline and cannot abuse an aircraft like the airlines do with quick turnarounds, cargo

holds packed with baggage and sometimes inexperienced groundcrew working in less than ideal conditions.

Still, in a testament to the rigorous test programme and service-ready philosophy, the 777 had an impressive performance in its first year, achieving a respectable 97.7% dispatch reliability while averaging 12hr of flying a day each. This industry measure shows the percentage of times an aircraft leaves the boarding gate within 15min of schedule, free from mechanical delays. It took the 767 18 months and 747-400 38 months to reach the same level of reliability.

The one-year anniversary also marked some milestones in Everett: the 50th 777 was being built for delivery to ANA in December 1996; production had started on the first variant, the 777-200IGW; and the design for the stretched 777, the -300 model, was 25% complete.

By August 1996, WA001, the first 777, had logged 1,440 flight hours in 556 flights for testing, crew training for airlines and demonstration tours. This last task in particular kept the aircraft busy — from June 1995 to June 1996, the aircraft travelled more than 60,000 miles around the globe. The 777 went abroad in September 1995, on a 11,729nm tour of Europe with stops in Geneva, Warsaw, Vienna, London and Frankfurt.

A tour of Latin America followed in March 1996, with stops in Mexico City, Bogota,

Santiago, Buenos Aires, São Paulo, Rio de Janeiro and San Salvador. This was an important market for Boeing to pitch its jet at. The company projects air travel in the region will grow by 5.6% per year over the next two decades, creating a demand for new aircraft worth $44 billion.

It was also a busy year for sales staff as the 777 order book swelled to 268 orders from 20 air carriers. Boeing was claiming it had captured 75% of the market since the aircraft's launch in October 1990.

On 18 June 1995, Boeing sealed a whopper of a sale: Saudi Arabian Airlines (Saudia) announced plans to buy 23 777-

200s and five 747-400s in a deal worth $5.2 billion. Deliveries of the jets, powered by GE90 engines, began in 1997.

August saw EgyptAir place an order for three Boeing 777-200 IGW models for delivery in 1997. The aircraft will have PW4090 engines rated at 90,000lb thrust.

In November, South African Airways said it was going to buy four of the higher gross weight 777-200s and take options for three more to be used on some of the airline's longer routes to Europe and the Middle East.

That same month brought another huge deal for both Boeing and Rolls-Royce when Singapore Airlines announced it would order 36 777s and place options for an additional 43, a deal valued at $12.7 billion. Six of the orders and 10 options would be held by Singapore Aircraft Leasing Enterprise, the leasing associate of the airline. Deliveries will start in 1997 through to 2004 to replace some Airbus A310s and older 747s. The orders were for the base model powered by the Trent 800 but the airline had the right to substitute other variants. In particular, Singapore was said to be interested in both the 777-300 and the super long-range 777-100X, capable of flying routes nonstop not previously possible, such as Singapore-Los Angeles. The following year started strong for the 777 Division when Malaysia Airlines ordered 15 777-200s and 300s and options for two more, all powered by Rolls-Royce engines.

In March 1996, International Lease Finance Corp ordered 18 777s, adding to its original order for six of the twinjets in 1992. The order was for both IGW models and -300s with the final mix to be decided later. Deliveries will start in 1999 through to 2004.

The 777 order book swelled further that summer with a decision by Garuda Indonesia in June to purchase six long-range 777-200s as part of a bigger order for 23 Boeing aircraft worth $1.6 billion. Kuwait Airways ordered two IGW models worth $280 million. Boeing got more good news in August. United Airlines announced it would be adding two more 777s to its fleet, part of a bigger order worth $3.5 billion that also included 19 747s.

November 1996 proved to be a banner month for the aircraft, starting with an order on 20 November from Air France for 10 IGW models to be powered by GE90 engines. The French carrier will get its first 777 in 1998, configured to seat 288 in three classes. The 777 purchase replaces a previous order for seven 767-300s and eight 737-500s. Air France said it needed more long-range aircraft and would use the 777s on its high-capacity routes, such as the North Atlantic.

Boeing confirmed the following day that American Airlines, one of the airlines that had helped design the 777, had ordered 12 777-200s to be delivered between 1998 and 2001.

The 777s were part of a blockbuster deal valued at $6.5 billion that made Boeing the

sole supplier of jets to the airline for the next 20 years. American announced firm orders for 103 jets by 2001, with 'purchase rights' for 527 more aircraft, including 38 more 777s. These rights give the airline greater flexibility to take on new aircraft as needed.

Asiana Airlines of South Korea rounded out the banner year with an order for seven 777-200s and eight 777-300s. Early plans called for the aircraft to be powered by Pratt & Whitney PW4098 and 4090 engines.

The year ended as one of the best ever for Boeing with announced orders for 717 aircraft worth $53 billion, including orders for 90 777s worth $12.7 billion. The boom reversed several years of declining revenues, deliveries, employment and profit and marked a dramatic turnabout from the early days of the 777 programme.

Top:
Blue skies provide a nice backdrop for this Emirates 777. The airline introduced the 777 to the Middle East in June 1995, flying it to Europe and Australia from United Arab Emirates. The airline had ordered seven 777s. *Emirates*

Above:
Dubbed the 'Rainbow 777', the paint scheme of this Japan Air System 777 was the brainchild of a 13-year-old Japanese boy. His design was picked over 10,000 other entrants in the airline's contest to design a new livery. The aircraft, configured to seat 380 in three classes, flies domestic routes in Japan. *Boeing*

In response, Boeing increased production rates for all models and at some points was hiring 1,500 new employees a month just to stay ahead of demand.

777 Family

It was Boeing's intent from the launch of the 777 programme to develop the aircraft as a family of jetliners, capitalizing on the airframe's flexibility and the huge thrust potential of the new engines.

Following that concept, the company introduced three versions of the 777: the base model, the transcontinental 777-200; the intercontinental 777-200IGW capable of carrying additional fuel to fly longer routes; and the 777-300, a stretched version able to seat up to 550 passengers in an all-economy configuration.

Two other variants are also under study: the smaller 777-100X, an ultra long-range model that could fly farther than the 747-400; and the 777-200X, which would combine the longer range of the -100X with the larger capacity of the -200.

777-200

The 777-200 has a range of maximum take-off weights to offer airlines flexibility to match specific routes and payload requirements with higher thrust engines providing the extra performance.

At its initial maximum gross weight of 506,000lb, the aircraft has a range of 4,350nm. Two optional higher weights of 515,000lb and 545,000lb are offered with engines rated at 74,000lb to 77,000lb thrust. The base model had an original maximum gross weight of 535,000lb. Engineers however boosted that by an extra 10,000lb when the results of flight testing and static and fatigue testing showed the aircraft could handle the additional weight. A 31,000gal fuel capacity allows ranges approaching 5,000nm, ideal for flights between the US east coast and Europe. It seats 305 to 328 passengers in a three-class arrangement, 375-400 in two classes.

The -200 model is well-suited for routes that are too big for the 767 and yet too small to be economically served by a 747-400.

It is a niche that Boeing is continuing to

develop with its announcement in early 1997 that it was offering the 767-400ERX, an aircraft sized between the 767-300 and the 777-200. The aircraft's stretched fuselage would seat 10-15% more passengers than the 767-300 — accommodating 303 in a two-class set-up compared to 269 in the -300. With a maximum take-off weight of 440,000lb, it would have a range of about 5,525nm. First delivery is tentatively scheduled for 2000 if the company gets enough orders.

777-200IGW

The 777-200 Increased Gross Weight shares the same dimensions as the base model but flies farther and has a higher maximum take-off weight thanks to greater fuel capacity and higher thrust engines.

This model, dubbed the B-market, is capable of take-off weights of 580,000lb to 632,500lb using engines rated at 84,000lb and 90,000lb thrust. This variant also has a larger centre tank, allowing it to carry

Above:
The second 777-200 increased gross weight model for British Airways nears completion on the assembly line. The jet has the same dimensions as the base model but increased fuel capacity and higher gross weights enable it to fly 2,000nm farther. *Author*

45,220gal of fuel, 14,220gal more than the base model.

The 777-200IGW has a seating capacity similar to the base model but will fly routes of 5,960nm to 7,230nm, enough for nonstop flights between city pairs such as London and Los Angeles and Tokyo and Sydney.

The higher gross weight model was proving popular with the airlines and it was outselling the base model by a margin of more than two to one.

The first IGW flew in October 1996 in the colours of British Airways, its launch customer. Within weeks, the aircraft was flown at its maximum take-off weight of 632,500lb, the highest gross weight yet for the 777. Boeing was also offering an increase in the aircraft's maximum gross weight to 648,000lb, an option that would extend its range to 7,500nm. The aircraft would require the reinforced landing gear used on the 777-300 and thicker wing gauge to handle the higher weight.

Boeing was to deliver the first GE-powered IGW model to British Airways in February 1997; a Pratt & Whitney-powered model to United Airlines in March and a Rolls-Royce Trent 890 version to Emirates in April.

777-300

Just a week after the first 777-200s entered revenue service, Boeing announced at the 1995 Paris Air Show that it had commitments worth $3.1 billion from Asian carriers for 31 stretched versions of the 777. Two weeks later, Boeing's Board of Directors gave the formal go-ahead for the development of the 777-300.

The 777-300 is known by some airlines as 'the people mover'. It can carry 20% more passengers than the smaller -200 model: 368 to 394 in three-class; 451-479 in two-class and up to 550 in an all-economy configuration. With a fuel capacity of 45,220gal, the 777-300 will have a range of 5,380nm.

A 210in fuselage plug added ahead of the wing and another 189in plug behind stretches the new aircraft to 242ft, beating the -200 by 33ft to become the world's largest twin-engine commercial jetliner. It's even longer than the 747-400 by 17ft. An extra door is added to each side above the wing.

The initial 777-300s will be powered by the same 90,000lb thrust engines used on the 777-200IGW. Boeing however expects even higher thrust needs for the jet and is designing the body, wing and tail to handle 98,000lb of thrust.

Designed for short to medium length routes in high density markets, the 777-300 is ideal for the Asian markets, as shown by the order book. At the Paris Air Show, All Nippon announced that it was taking 10 of the -300s for use on flights between Tokyo and destinations in Western Europe and the west coast of North America. Korean Air Lines ordered four 777-300s and converted another four of its previous order for eight 777s. Thai International said it would buy six -300s in addition to the eight basic versions already ordered. Of the commitments announced at the show, 20 were for new orders and 11 were confirmations or conversions of earlier orders for the 777-200.

Cathay Pacific converted seven of its 11 777 orders to the stretched model and became the launch customer for the aircraft. Roll-out was scheduled for August 1997. Three of the jets would be used for the flight test programme and first delivery to Cathay is slated for May 1998 with deliveries to other airlines later that year.

The stretched version is a natural evolution of the base model and is expected to be a popular replacement for the older model 747s. The 777-300 will have similar passenger capacity and range as the 747-100s and -200s but will burn one-third less fuel and its maintenance costs will be 40% lower for an overall operating cost that is one-third less. Boeing's venerable long-hauler, the 747-400, will continue to dominate the long-range,

Comparison of the 777 Stretch and the 777-200

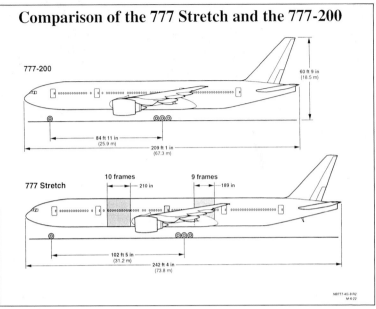

777-200

60 ft 9 in
(18.5 m)

84 ft 11 in
(25.9 m)

209 ft 1 in
(67.3 m)

10 frames
210 in

9 frames
189 in

777 Stretch

102 ft 5 in
(31.2 m)

242 ft 4 in
(73.8 m)

NB777 4/G-8 R2
M-6-22

higher capacity routes. But the 777-300 will find a niche for medium range, high density routes such as Tokyo to Singapore, San Francisco to Tokyo or Honolulu to Seoul.

The two fuselage plugs are placed in the middle of the forward and aft cargo holds, adding 33ft of extra cargo space. This boosts volume in the front hold by 33% and 43% in the rear.

The stretch adds another 18ft to the 84ft wheelbase of the 777-200, presenting a challenge for the pilots tasked with negotiating narrow taxiways and crowded airport ramps. To assist ground manoeuvring and help keep pilots out of the grass, the -300 will be equipped with three cameras, two on the horizontal stabilizer pointing forward towards each main gear bogey and another on the aircraft's belly showing the nose landing gear. The images will be displayed in the cockpit so the pilots can see exactly where the gear are tracking during taxying. And because of its longer length, the -300 will have a tailskid.

Future Variants

Boeing and the engine makers are in discussions with airlines about the potential of 777 models with greater payload and range performance and more powerful

engines. Boeing has always built big wings with plenty of growth potential. Key to the growth of the 777 is its huge wing which can handle increases in gross weight up to 720,000lb. Any further weight increases would require significant changes to the wing structure.

This creates the potential for the 777-200X, which will probably be the next development of the 777 with even greater range than the -200IGW. This C-market model would have dimensions similar to the base aircraft but its maximum take-off weight would be between 690,000lb and 720,000lb. The heavier jet would be powered by 98,000lb thrust engines and a fuel capacity of 46,680 US gallons would give it the ability to carry 305 passengers about 8,500nm. Wingtip extension would increase the wingspan by 4.5ft to create more lift and improve cruise performance. With its higher gross weight and a seating capacity roughly comparable to the

777-200 model, the -200X would combine good economics and greater range to serve medium-density, very-long-range markets. The aircraft would require strengthened portions of the wing and centre fuselage, stronger tyres and brakes and a beefed-up landing gear to handle the higher weights. The jet would also have provision for additional fuel capacity in the form of tanks loaded in the aft cargo compartment.

Boeing was also considering a 'shrink' of the 777-200, called the -100X, to serve very-long-range routes. The aircraft would be 12 frames and 21ft shorter than the 777-200 but would have a high gross weight and powerful engines. This would give it potential for huge range for direct, nonstop service between new city pairs. Operating at 660,000lb — the same as the 777-300 — and with power-plants capable of 98,000lb thrust, the -100 would carry 250 passengers 8,500nm, enough to permit nonstop flights between virtually any two cities.

The -100X though would only be good for ultra-long-range markets and would be uneconomical to operate on shorter flights. As shown by the limited success of the 747SP, of which only 45 were sold, airlines are reluctant to buy aircraft designed for very restricted markets. For that reason, development of the -100X had slowed by the autumn of 1996 and Boeing was devoting its efforts to the more promising -200X derivative. Also being talked about was the -300X, a heavier version

of the 777-300 that would have a gross weight of 690,000lb. This would allow extra fuel to increase the aircraft's range by an additional 400 to 500nm, up to about 6,000nm. The wing's remarkable ability could also support a 710,000lb version of the -300 but would require engines of 105,000lb thrust.

The -200X programme got a boost in early 1997 when Boeing decided to halt development of the 'superjumbo' versions of the 747 because of a lack of orders. Ironically, it was the success of aircraft like the 777 and 767 that forced the decision. With the popularity of twinjets like these, air traffic has been shifting away from larger hub cities to more thinly travelled city pairs. Boeing officials said that airlines today are more likely to 'fragment' their routes, using smaller aircraft for nonstop flights from mid-sized cities, rather than consolidating routes in hubs. As a result, Boeing said it wanted to concentrate on longer-range derivatives of its twins, the 767 and the 777.

By the end of 1996, 45 777s had been delivered to nine airlines around the world. The following year, 1997, promises to be another big year in the evolution of the 777 family with the first deliveries of the IGW models and the first flight of the 777-300 in the autumn. The success of the 777 guarantees the aircraft will be an increasingly familiar sight at world airports in years to come.

Appendix I:
Specifications

	777-200	777-300
Dimensions		
Length	209ft 1in	242ft 4in
Wingspan	199ft 11in	199ft 11in
Tail height	60ft 9in	60ft 8in
Fuselage diameter	20ft 4in	20ft 4in
Cabin cross-section	19ft 3in	19ft 3in
Seating Capacity*		
Three-class	305-328	368-394
Two-class	375-400	451-479
All-economy	418-440	up to 550
Cargo Capacity		
Containers	32 LD-3s	Eight pallet containers and 20 LD-3s
Bulk cargo	600cu ft	600cu ft
Total volume	5,656cu ft	7,080cu ft
Maximum Take-off Weights		
Initial models	506,000lb	660,000lb
	515,000lb	
	545,000lb	
Increased Gross		
Weight Models	580,000lb	N/A
	590,000lb	
	632,500lb	
Range		
Initial Models	3,780nm	5,380nm
	4,050nm	
	4,930nm	
Increased Gross		
Weight Models	5,960nm	N/A
	6,220nm	
	7,230nm	
Fuel Capacity		
Initial Models	31,000gal	45,220gal
Increased Gross		
Weight Models	45,220gal	N/A
Engines	PW 4074, 4077, 4084, 4090	PW 4090, 4098
	GE90 -75, -76, -85, -90	GE90-92
	Trent 875, 877, 884, 890	Trent 892, 895

* Seating variation depends on airline's choice of nine or 10-abreast seating in economy and seven or eight-abreast seating in business class.

Appendix II:
Performance Data for 777-200 with PW4077 Engines

Take-off

Maximum take-off weight	545,000lb
Maximum zero fuel weight	420,000lb
Operating empty weight	303,600lb
Maximum payload	116,400lb
Passengers	305
Take-off field length	8,400ft (sea level, 86° F)
Take-off thrust	77,200lb per engine

Cruise

Cruise mach	0.84
Design range	5,250nm
Maximum speed	0.87
Ceiling at MTOW	36,800ft
Max certificated ceiling	43,100ft
Engine out ceiling	15,900ft

Landing

Maximum landing weight	445,000lb
Approach speed at MLW	136kt
Landing field length	5,100ft

Systems
Hydraulics

Number of independent systems	Three
Number of independent pumps	Nine
System pressure	3,000psi
Type of pumps	Two engine-driven
	Four electrical
	Two air-driven
	RAT pump

Electrical power

Number of ac generators	Six	
Location and capacity	Engine	two at 120kVA
		two back-up at 20kVA
	APU 120kVA	
	RAT 7.5kVA	
Transformer rectifier units	Five	

Auxiliary power unit

Model	Allied Signal Engines 331-500
Operational altitudes	Pneumatic power to 22,000ft
	Electrical power to 43,100ft
Maximum in-flight start altitude	43,100ft

Appendix III:
Boeing 777 Orders

as of 31 December 1996

Airline Customer	Engines	Total	
Air France	GE	10	
All Nippon Airways	PW	28	includes 10 777-300s
American Airlines	-	12	
Asiana Airlines	PW	15	includes 8 777-300s
British Airways	GE	18	
Cathay Pacific	RR	11	includes 7 777-300s
China Southern	GE	6	
Continental Airlines	GE	5	
Egyptair	PW	3	
Emirates	RR	7	
Garuda Indonesia	-	6	
GE Capital Aviation Services	GE	5	
ILFC	GE/RR/PW	24	
Japan Air System	PW	7	
Japan Airlines	PW	15	includes 5 777-300s
Korean Air	PW	12	includes 8 777-300s
Kuwait Airways	GE	2	
Lauda Air	GE	4	
Malaysia Airlines	RR	15	includes 5 777-300s
Saudi Arabian Airlines	GE	23	
Singapore Airlines	RR	36	
South African Airways	-	4	
Thai Airways Int'l	RR	14	includes 6 777-300s
United Airlines	PW	36	
Total		318	

Appendix IV
777 Construction List

Line No	Serial No	Model No	First Operator	Registration	Delivery
1	27116	200	Boeing	N7771	-
2	26936	222	United AL	N774UA	29/03/96
3	26932	222	United AL	N771UA	27/11/95
4	26929	222	United AL	N773UA	31/01/96
5	26930	222	United AL	N772UA	29/09/95
6	27105	236	British AW	G-ZZZA	20/05/96
7	26916	222	United AL	N777UA	15/05/95
8	26917	222	United AL	N766UA	24/05/95
9	26918	222	United AL	N767UA	31/05/95
10	27106	236	British AW	G-ZZZB	28/03/95
11	26919	222	United AL	N768UA	26/06/95
12	26921	222	United AL	N769UA	27/06/95
13	26925	222	United AL	N770UA	13/07/95
14	27265	267	Cathay Pacific	VR-HNA	23/08/96
15	27107	236	British AW	G-ZZZC	11/11/95
16	27027	281	All Nippon	JA8197	04/10/95
17	27108	236	British AW	G-ZZZD	28/12/95
18	27266	267	Cathay Pacific	VR-HNB	25/10/96

Line No	Serial No	Model No	First Operator	Registration	Delivery
19	27109	236	British AW	G-ZZZE	12/01/96
20	27357	21B	China Southern	B-2051	30/12/95
21	27028	281	All Nippon	JA8198	20/12/95
22	26947	222	United AL	N775UA	22/01/96
23	27364	246	Japan AL	JA8981	15/02/96
24	27358	21B	China Southern	B-2052	29/02/96
25	27726	2D7	Thai Int'l	HS-TJA	31/03/96
26	27365	246	Japan AL	JA8982	28/03/96
27	26937	222	United AL	N776UA	10/04/96
28	27263	267	Cathay Pacific	VR-HNC	09/05/96
29	27029	281	All Nippon	JA8199	23/05/96
30	27247	21H	Emirates	A6-EMD	05/06/96
31	27264	267	Cathay Pacific	VR-HND	13/06/96
32	27727	2D7	Thai Int'l	HS-TJB	13/06/96
33	27248	21H	Emirates	A6-EME	03/07/96
34	26940	222	United AL	N778UA	18/07/96
35	26941	222	United AL	N779UA	26/07/96
36	26944	222	United AL	N780UA	06/08/96
37	27030	281	All Nippon	JA8967	12/08/96
38	27031	281	All Nippon	JA8968	14/08/96
39	27366	246	Japan AL	JA8983	12/09/96
40	26945	222	United AL	N781UA	12/09/96
41	27483	236IGW	British AW	G-VIIA	01/07/97*
42	27249	21H	Emirates	A6-EMF	16/10/96
43	26939	222IGW	United AL	N787UA	01/06/97*
44	27728	2D7	Thai Int'l	HS-TJC	25/10/96
45	27636	289	Japan Air System	JA8977	03/12/96
46	27359	21B	China Southern	B-2053	15/11/96
47	27250	21HIGW	Emirates	A6-EMI	01/07/97*
48	27360	21B	China Southern	B-2054	27/11/96
49	27484	236IGW	British AW	G-VIIB	01/05/97*
50	27032	281	All Nippon	JA8969	16/12/96
51	27729	2D7	Thai Int'l	HS-TJD	19/12/96
52	26938	222IGW	United AL	N786UA	04/04/97
53	27485	236IGW	British AW	G-VIIC	06/02/97
54	27251	21HIGW	Emirates	A6-EMH	01/05/97*
55	27524	21BIGW	China Southern	B-2055	28/02/97
56	27486	236IGW	British AW	G-VIID	18/02/97
57	26948	222IGW	United AL	N782UA	07/03/97
58	27487	236IGW	British AW	G-VIIE	27/02/97
59	27945	2B5IGW	Korean Air	HL7530	21/03/97
60	26950	222IGW	United AL	N783UA	11/03/97
61	27488	236IGW	British AW	G-VIIF	19/03/97
62	27946	2B5IGW	Korean Air	HL7531	28/03/97
63	27252	21HIGW	Emirates	A6-EMG	01/04/97*
64	28408	2H6IGW	Malaysian AL	9M-MRA	23/04/97
65	27489	236IGW	British AW	G-VIIG	04/97*
66	27525	21BIGW	China Southern	B-2056	01/04/97*
67	-	212IGW	Singapore AL	-	01/05/97*
68	27651	246	Japan AL	JA8984	01/04/97*
69	26951	222IGW	United AL	N784UA	01/04/97*
70	27490	236IGW	British AW	G-VIIH	01/05/97*
71	-	266IGW	Egyptair	-	01/05/97*
72	27652	246	Japan AL	JA8985	01/05/97*
73	26954	222IGW	United AL	N785UA	01/05/97*
74	28409	2H6IGW	Malaysian AL	9M-MRB	01/05/97*
75	27033	281	All Nippon	-	01/06/97*

* tentative delivery schedule. IGW — Increased Gross Weight models